Financial Freedom

A Step-by-Step Practical Guide for Walking in God's Blessings

By Terry Dean

Unless otherwise indicated, all Scripture quotations are taken from the King James Version of the Bible.

Scripture taken from THE AMPLIFIED BIBLE, Old Testament copyright © 1965, 1987 by the Zondervan Corporation. The Amplified New Testament copyright © 1958, 1987 by the Lockman Foundation. Used by permission.

Any underlining in Scriptures has been added for special emphasis by the publisher.

Personal pronouns referring to God the Father, God the Son, or God the Holy Spirit have always been capitalized throughout this book as special recognition of God.

Financial Freedom
Copyright © 2004, 2006 by Terry Dean

ISBN 0-9778671-0-2

Published By:

MyMarketingCoach, LLC
2747 South County Road 600 East
New Castle, IN 47362
http://www.mymarketingcoach.com

Printed in the United States of America. All rights reserved under International Copyright Law. Contents and/or cover may not be reproduced in whole or in part without express written consent of the publisher.

"This publication is designed to provide general information in regard to the subject matter covered. It is sold with the understanding that the publisher is not engaged in rendering legal, accounting, or other professional services. If legal, accounting, or other professional services are required, the services of an independent professional should be sought. From the declaration of principles jointly adopted by a committee of the American Bar Association and the committee of the Publisher's Association." Products sold as is, with all faults, without warranties of any kind, either express or implied, including, but not limited to, the implied warranties of merchantability and fitness for a particular purpose.

Table of Contents

Introduction	5
1 One Word from God Can Change Your Life Forever	9
2 God Has Always Provided Wealth for His People	19
3 The Wealth of the Wicked is Laid Up for the Righteous	38
4 Was Jesus Poor?	51
5 Jesus Became Poor so You Could Become Rich	64
6 The Giving Heart of a Son	86
7 What About the Hundredfold Return?	97
8 How to Give God's Way	112
9 Tithing…By Law or By Grace	123
10 Waiting For a Miracle and Missing Your Blessing	134
11 The Grasshopper Complex	141
12 Our Strength Comes From Praise	159
13 Practical Wisdom for Daily Living	171
14 More Practical Wisdom for Daily Living	185
15 Finding God's Road of Success for You	199
16 How to Become Financially Free from Debt	210
17 Find Your Passion…And You'll Realize Your Purpose	220
18 Meditate in the Word	243

Introduction

Money is one of the most debated topics in the church world today. Some Christians feel we should go through life poor desperately awaiting heaven when all of our problems will finally be over. They feel God has promised to just barely meet our needs and we're destined to go through life just barely making it. They say that if we have just enough food to make it through today without starving, then we're doing well.

This concept has consumed the minds of the church all throughout history. Go back a few hundred years and it was the common wisdom of the day that you should give away all your possessions and lock yourself away in a monastery if you wanted to be holy and find God. They felt all money was evil and you were better off if you had nothing to do with it.

Nothing could be further from the truth. Throughout the last couple of decades God has been revealing to the church money is not evil. It is a tool that when used correctly can bring millions to a saving knowledge of Jesus Christ. Money is neither good nor evil on its own. It is simply a tool. It can be used to sin or it can be used to bless people. It's all up to the character of the owner.

Over the past few years we've learned some incredible truths from Scriptures which have been hidden for centuries:

> *"But thou shalt remember the LORD thy God: for it is he that giveth thee power to get wealth, that he may establish his covenant which he sware unto thy fathers, as it is this day."*
> Deuteronomy 8:18

> *"A good man leaveth an inheritance to his children's children: and the wealth of the sinner is laid up for the just."*
> Proverbs 13:22

"For ye know the grace of our Lord Jesus Christ, that, though he was rich, yet for your sakes he became poor, that ye through his poverty might be rich."
2 Corinthians 8:9

All of these verses show God wants more for us than just getting by. He desires for us to walk in His full blessings. He doesn't want us to be in debt. A banker shouldn't have the ability to tell the church what we can or cannot do for God. God has promised financial blessings to the church, and we are finally learning what has been made available to us.

The only problem is that some of these valuable truths have been taken out of context. They have been taken to extremes at times by ministers and have been used to beat the sheep to death and at times even financial ruin. They have introduced a new form of legalism into the church where many Christians have been taught the only way to receive from God is to give to a few "select" ministers.

So while the pure truth of God's desire for us to be blessed has brought freedom to millions of Christians, the misuse of certain Bible verses and overemphasis on legalistic giving has caused pain for many others. The goal of this book is to teach you the truth about finances, to show you God's desire to see you blessed, and to fully explain the Scriptures on finances and giving.

Here are just a few of things you will learn throughout this book:

Why God Wants to Bless You with Financial Abundance...

How YOU can Get Fully Out of Debt...Even Your Mortgage...

How to Break the Power of Poverty Thinking in Your Life...

Why You May Be Giving and Giving and Never Seeing a Return...

How to Give GOD'S WAY and Be Blessed for It Every Time...

How to Become Financially Free Straight Out of Proverbs...

How to Spot Religious Scams Out to Take You For Every Penny...

Why Tithing can be a legalistic bondage or a Doorway to Freedom...

How to Receive God's Blessings in Your Finances Every Day...

How to Break the Spirit of Debt in Your Life Forever...

How to Give More Money Away Than Many People Earn...

If you pay attention, you will learn all this and more throughout this book. Isn't it time that you stop living from paycheck to paycheck? Isn't it time that you were able to provide the best clothing, schooling, and opportunities for your children? Isn't it time for you to be able to give those offerings you would really like to be giving to your church?

It is time...and this is your opportunity. You're going to finally learn how to stop praying for financial miracles and live in daily financial abundance. Instead of you praying for a miracle, you can be the one who is writing the check and providing financial miracles to others.

One of my goals in writing this book is to find 1,000,000 Christians who will stand up and claim the prosperity God has for them. I want to help one million people learn to become the champions God has created them to be. Will you be one of these people? I hope you will. It's your choice…and today is the day to make a decision to change your life forever.

Don't just speed read through this book. Sit down, take notes, use a highlighter, and spend time praying over what you're being taught. Read the chapters in order. Each chapter builds on the one before it in a line upon line and precept upon precept format. If you jump around or to the end of the book, you won't have a good understanding of the complete teaching.

You may have read "prosperity" books before and they may have been sent to your shelf never to be seen again. Let this book be a turning point in your life. Make a commitment to yourself, to your family, and to God that you are going to learn what God has to say about your finances once and for all. Decide that today is going to be the beginning of a new day in your life. From now on, you will never allow religious teachings to hold you back from everything God has provided for you.

This is your chance to learn the truth, and the truth will set you FREE.

This is the whole point of what is being taught here. It is all about you receiving REAL FINANCIAL FREEDOM which simply means having all your needs met, having money to buy what you want, and having enough left over to bless and provide financial miracles for others.

Chapter One
One Word From God Can Change Your Life Forever

It has been five years since the day my life changed forever. At the time of this writing I have been married and ordained for 10 years (we were married and ordained on the same day), but the first five years of our lives together were a financial disaster.

At that time we were living in a small rental house in Richmond, Indiana. There were leaks in the ceiling in the kitchen and the bathroom was full of water damage that had not been repaired by the landlord for over a year. Like many young couples, we were in debt up to our eyeballs. We had one vehicle, a Chevy Astro minivan with a dent in the front right side.

We had around a dozen credit cards and almost all of them were completely maxed out. We were often borrowing money from one credit card to just barely pay the minimum payments on the others. I remember when we would spend time searching through all the furniture trying to find enough change to go out to eat at McDonald's. McDonald's was a special treat for us in those days.

We were both working at jobs on and off, but we never did find a decent job for either one of us. My wife has a Bachelor's degree, but the highest paying job she found with it was only $6.25 an hour. I've done all kinds of jobs including selling satellite dishes door-to-door, signing people up for credit cards in front of Sears, delivering pizzas for Little Caesar's, and even delivering newspapers (as an ordained minister at 22 years old).

I don't even want to imagine how bad our lives would have been if we had children at the time. Free time was spent studying the Bible, listening to ministry tapes, and preaching. We had a Bible study and church in our home during part of this time period.

The saddest part of this story was that we fully believed in prosperity. We believed the verses that teach God wanting to bless his people. We listened to tapes on prosperity. We read books on financial blessings. We believed in confession and fully believed that if we confessed the Word enough, our situation would change. It did finally change, but not in the way we expected or had been taught.

The most often quoted verse about financial blessings is this one:

> *"Give, and it shall be given unto you; good measure, pressed down, and shaken together, and running over, shall men give into your bosom. For with the same measure that ye mete withal it shall be measured to you again."*
> Luke 6:38

We knew that verse by heart and I quoted it regularly. You would be hard pressed to go to any charismatic church and not have that verse quoted at least several times during the service, especially at offering time. We believed and quoted that verse at almost every offering.

Another popular "financial" verse is this one:

> *"But he that received seed into the good ground is he that heareth the word, and understandeth it; which also beareth fruit, and bringeth forth, some an hundredfold, some sixty, some thirty."*
> Matthew 13:23

Because of this verse and the other ones similar to it, we constantly believed for a hundredfold return on our giving. It's too bad that this verse really isn't about money. It has been badly taken out of context and we will study it in context later on in this book.

We would give $500 to a ministry and go home confessing God was going to bless us with $50,000 (hundredfold return on the giving). In fact, I don't know how many times we gave away $500 exactly just because we were expecting and praying for that $50,000 return to get us out of our financial situation. We borrowed from our credit cards many times to make these gifts (yes, these are the same credit cards which were almost maxed out).

If you would have asked me at the time I would have even told you that many of these gifts were because God specifically told me to give them (and to expect the financial return). My wife and I fully believed that God was going to miraculously have some millionaire walk up to us one day and hand us or our ministry the check to get us out of our financial problems. That day never came in spite of all our giving.

God's deliverance for us came in a completely different way. Instead of sending us the miracle check, He gave me a revelation in my spirit. This one revelation changed our lives from that day forward. Our situation started changing for the better the same week. We were able to pay our bills on time. We soon started paying off our debts. We moved to a much nicer rental house. A year later we bought our own home with 18.5 acres. The loan for our home was paid off in less than ONE year.

We purchased two brand new vehicles with cash. We've been on a second honeymoon to Cancun (we never actually had a first honeymoon because we could never afford it). We have thousands of dollars invested in real estate. Last year we GAVE away more money than we used to earn in 3 years.

All of the above didn't come overnight. It is over several years. The changes began occurring immediately from the moment the revelation came. Instead of going deeper in debt, we started coming out of debt. I have learned quite a bit more about finances from the Bible since then, but that one revelation was the breakthrough for me.

We have gone from complete financial bondage to true financial freedom. Today we run our own businesses and also minister in churches instead of having to do whatever it took to just stay afloat. A banker doesn't tell me what I can or can't do for God. Money doesn't rule my life. It is simply a tool that works for me while I work for God.

This is true financial freedom…and it's what I want to share with you. I'm sure that by now you'd like to know what it was I learned that day. The revelation I received from God in my spirit was simply this:

"Don't pray for money anymore. Pray for wisdom and you'll never have trouble with money again."

It's a simple message, but it is life changing. The problem up until that point is we had constantly prayed for money over and over again. There were times we had received a small financial blessing here and there, but they never got us out of the problem. The problem was always there and continually got worse.

This will sound harsh to someone who may be in the same situation we were, but you've already made a commitment to changing your financial life. So here goes. The problem wasn't money. The problem was us. If God would have somehow dropped the money we were praying for down in our lap, it would have helped for a while. Within a year we would have gotten ourselves back into the same type of horrible situation. We would have then been praying for another financial miracle to break us out of our bondage again.

Nothing would have changed if we had received the money we had been praying for immediately. I wouldn't be writing this book now and I would still be in debt living in a cheap poorly taken care of rental house somewhere. Besides that, it would have been IMPOSSIBLE for God to provide us with the money the way we were expecting to receive it. I can hear some of you screaming, "WHAT?" after that last sentence. Yes, I said it would have been IMPOSSIBLE for God to have answered our prayer in the way we were expecting.

Now I know what you are thinking. You are probably thinking that NOTHING IS IMPOSSIBLE FOR GOD. That is correct with one exception. It is impossible for God to lie. He cannot lie. It is against His very nature to ever lie.

> *"In hope of eternal life, which God, that cannot lie, promised before the world began;"*
> Titus 1:2

What does this have to do with our prayers you may ask? It is simple really. We were praying for financial blessings, yet there were areas in our life that guaranteed we would stay poor. Throughout the Bible God gives very specific instructions about how to become wealthy…and also how to stay poor. We were following HIS instructions for being poor in many situations.

God could not financially bless us until we started changing. Our mindset had to change. Our actions had to change. How and why we gave to others had to change. We had to learn God's divine wealth secrets. That is why we had to pray for wisdom. Wisdom would bring the wealth along with it.

> *"Through wisdom is an house builded; and by understanding it is established: And by knowledge shall the chambers be filled with all precious and pleasant riches."*
> Proverbs 24:3-4

> *"Wisdom is the principal thing; therefore get wisdom: and with all thy getting get understanding."*
> Proverbs 4:7

Wisdom is the principal thing. Principal here means, *"the first, in place, time, order, and rank."* Wisdom is the first thing you should be concentrating on. It is the important thing for you to concentrate on to change your life. Wisdom will bring you the money you want and need in your life. Wisdom is the "practical application of knowledge." It's knowing how to apply what you know to your daily life. You may have knowledge of a subject such as knowing or memorizing certain Bible verses, but do you know how to apply them to your daily life? That is wisdom.

How to Get Wisdom From God

The Scripture I received my revelation from was this one over in James:

> *"If any of you lack wisdom, let him ask of God, that giveth to all men liberally, and upbraideth not; and it shall be given him. But let him ask in faith, nothing wavering. For he that wavereth is like a wave of the sea driven with the wind and tossed. For let not that man think that he shall receive any thing of the Lord. A double minded man is unstable in all his ways."*
> James 1:5-8

God promises here He will give you wisdom liberally as long as you ask in faith with nothing wavering. This means you have to pray to God in faith without any doubt or unbelief. You simply believe when you pray that God will answer your prayer and provide you with the wisdom you need in your daily life.

There is a second step to receiving wisdom from God. You must pray and ask for it, but you must also study to receive knowledge. Since wisdom is knowing how to apply knowledge, it won't do you any good if you don't spend your time also studying the Word of God to find out what God tells you about your finances.

> *"For the LORD giveth wisdom: out of his mouth cometh knowledge and understanding."*
> Proverbs 2:6

Begin studying the Word of God to find out what God has to say about wisdom, foolishness, finances, business, real estate, jobs, giving, tithing, receiving, and every other subject that has to do with your financial life. Throughout this book you will be learning what God has taught me regarding wisdom and finances, but pray and study what has been provided for you here so you can receive the same revelation from God on this subject.

Who Else Prayed for Wisdom?

James chapter one tells us that we should all be praying for wisdom. Let's get a confirmation for this. Who else in the Bible prayed for wisdom instead of just praying for money?

> *"In that night did God appear unto Solomon, and said unto him, Ask what I shall give thee. And Solomon said unto God, Thou hast shewed great mercy unto David my father, and hast made me to reign in his stead. Now, O LORD God, let thy promise unto David my father be established: for thou hast made me king over a people like the dust of the earth in multitude. <u>Give me now wisdom</u> and knowledge, that I may go out and come in before this people: for who can judge this thy people, that is so great?"*
> II Chronicles 1:7-10

God showed up to Solomon and basically offered to give him anything he asked for. Solomon could have asked for fame for himself. He could have asked for the defeat of his enemies. He could have asked for money (like most of us do). No. Solomon didn't ask for any of that. He asked for wisdom. While most of us have spent years praying for money, Solomon didn't ask for that at all. He asked for wisdom…and let's take a look at what God's response to this was:

> *"And God said to Solomon, Because this was in thine heart, and thou hast not asked riches, wealth, or honour, nor the life of thine enemies, neither yet hast asked long life; but hast asked wisdom and knowledge for thyself, that thou mayest judge my people, over whom I have made thee king: Wisdom and knowledge is granted unto thee; and <u>I will give thee riches, and wealth, and honour,</u> such as none of the kings have had that have been before thee, neither shall there any after thee have the like."*
> 2 Chronicles 1:11-12

God answered Solomon's prayer and gave him wisdom and knowledge. Take notice of what ALSO came with the wisdom and knowledge. He received riches, and wealth, and honor to go along with the wisdom. All of these things are produced by wisdom! So if you want to receive them, you should be praying for wisdom yourself. What was the result of Solomon's prayer and God's blessing? Take a look:

> *"And all king Solomon's drinking vessels were of gold, and all the vessels of the house of the forest of Lebanon were of pure gold; none were of silver: it <u>was nothing accounted of</u> in the days of Solomon. For the king had at sea a navy of Tharshish with the navy of Hiram: once in three years came the navy of Tharshish, bringing gold, and silver, ivory, and apes, and peacocks. So king Solomon exceeded all the kings of the earth for riches and for wisdom. And all the earth sought to Solomon, to hear his wisdom, which God had put in his heart."*
> 1 Kings 10:21-24

All of the drinking vessels that Solomon owned were pure gold. All the vessels of the house were pure gold. Nothing was made of silver, because silver wasn't worth anything during Solomon's reign. That's a lot of gold. There was so much gold that silver didn't even have value anymore.

I've heard of some wealthy people, but I have never seen anything like that. Think about it. Bill Gates may be the richest man in the world, but he has nothing on Solomon. ALL the earth came to hear Solomon's wisdom. And we have someone greater than that in our midst today – Jesus!

That is God's desire for the church. He desires to fill us liberally with all wisdom so that the whole earth comes to us to hear our wisdom! In the past they have been making fun of us and saying that Christianity is just a crutch that poor people need. Well, times are changing. The Gospel must be preached in the entire world and receiving God's wisdom is the way to do it.

I know this kind of talk offends some people. They don't want to ask God for too much, and they don't even realize they are just being selfish. That's right. Only asking God for just enough money for you and yours to get by is selfish. God has given us a mission to do and it's not to sit in caves waiting for the end.

We are called to preach the Gospel to the world and it is going to take a lot of money to do this. So you don't need money just for yourself. You need money to finance missionary trips. You need money to feed all the poor in your city. You need money to pay your minister a good salary.

You are called to be God's gateway of finances on this earth. That's why you are interested in this subject. That's why you picked up this book. God doesn't print money in heaven and He doesn't rain it down on the earth. He uses men and women filled with His wisdom to go out and get the money to finance His kingdom.

"A good man leaveth an inheritance to his children's children: and the wealth of the sinner is laid up for the just."
Proverbs 13:22

The wealth of the sinner is being saved up for the just. Do you think they will just hand it over? No way. You are called to go out there and earn it using the wisdom of God. That's why you must pray for God's wisdom every day, and begin studying exactly what God has to say about money all throughout the Bible.

This book will give you the basic knowledge you need, but the wisdom only comes from God. So begin praying for wisdom today in faith...and never doubt for one second that He is filling you with more of His limitless storehouse of wisdom every single day of your life.

Chapter Two
God Has Always Provided Wealth for His People

God is not against His people having money. He has never been against it in spite of what you may have heard many preachers say. He is against money having them and ruling their lives. Remember this. Money is a great servant, but it is a horrible master.

> *"Therefore take no thought, saying, What shall we eat? or, What shall we drink? or, Wherewithal shall we be clothed? (For after all these things do the Gentiles seek:) for your heavenly Father knoweth that ye have need of all these things. But seek ye first the kingdom of God, and his righteousness; and <u>all these things shall be added unto you.</u>"*
> Matthew 6:31-33

You are to be seeking first the kingdom of God and then God promises that all these "things" will be added unto you. What kind of things is he talking about? He's talking about all the things the Gentiles seek! He is talking about food, drink, clothing, and all the other things the Gentiles are seeking. He has promised to take care of you as long as you put His kingdom first place in your life.

God has always taken care of His chosen people as long as they put Him first in their lives. The Bible is full of examples we can go to and show God's will for our lives and the wealth He desires to provide for us. Notice I used the term wealth. He doesn't desire to just give us enough to get barely by. He desires to take abundant care of us if we let Him.

Throughout the Old Testament God often used the name of El Shaddai for Himself…"The God Who Is More Than Enough." He never called himself "El Cheapo" or "The God of Barely Getting By." He is the God of MORE than enough. He is the God of Too Much.

> *"Thou preparest a table before me in the presence of mine enemies: thou anointest my head with oil; <u>my cup runneth over</u>."*
> Psalms 23:5

He wants to prepare a feast for us in the presence of our enemies. You may have heard that refers to heaven, but it can't. You don't have any enemies in heaven. Your enemies are here including Satan and his demons. God wants to provide you with a feast right in front of them where they can see you.

Even better, God says that *"my cup runneth over."* In other words, God wants to fill up your cup and just keep right on pouring. Take a glass out of your cupboard. Put it on the counter and start pouring water into it. Pour it right to the top and keep right on pouring. You'll make a mess all over the place. It will pour all over the counter and start dripping onto the floor. That is how God wants to bless you. He wants to bless you so much that it fills up everything you can take and it starts pouring all over everyone around you. Let's give another example to show you this isn't an isolated incident. It is God's way of doing things.

> *"Bring ye all the tithes into the storehouse, that there may be meat in mine house, and prove me now herewith, saith the LORD of hosts, if I will not open you the windows of heaven, and pour you out a blessing, that <u>there shall not be room enough</u> to receive it."*
> Malachi 3:10

God is promising to pour out a blessing that there is not enough room to receive it all. Does that sound like God wants to provide you with just enough to barely get by? No way! He wants to provide you with way more than enough. He wants to give you abundance so you have more than enough to share with and meet the needs of all those around you.

> *"Now unto him that is able to do <u>exceeding abundantly above</u> all that we ask or think, according to the power that worketh in us,"*
> Ephesians 3:20

God is able to do exceeding abundantly above all we can ask or even think. And if you're like me, you can think about a lot! God says He can do more than you can even think. So you can't outthink God for your life. His plan for you is already bigger than you can imagine. It is bigger than you can conceive of right now.

"Exceeding" means, "over, above, beyond, very chiefest, exceeding." "Abundantly above" is "huperekchuno" in the Greek and means, "to pour out over, overflow." God wants to go beyond overflowing your cup in this verse. In the Old Testament God wanted to provide overflowing blessings to His people. Now in our New Covenant God wants to go exceedingly beyond overflowing your cup!

We are in a New Covenant that God has established upon better promises than the Old Covenant. God wants to go far beyond what He did for His Old Testament saints for you. There is only one problem...Ephesians 3:20 above says,"it is according to the power that works in US." It is up to us to let Him work. God is limited to what you allow Him to do in your life. Let's take that one step further. God is limited to what you allow Him to do THROUGH you. You are His hands on this earth. He is limited to what you allow Him to do through you as His hands.

That is the key. God wants to bless you exceedingly abundantly to more than overflowing, but He is limited in your life by what you allow Him to do through you. He does not work apart from you. Jesus is the head of the church and we are the body. The head does not accomplish anything without the body taking action. The head gives direction and the body follows that direction.

What if your own natural body decided it didn't want to listen to the head anymore? What if you woke up one morning and told your body to get out of bed, but it decided it was on strike and wasn't going to listen anymore. You'd be stuck there paralyzed. Well, that is where much of the church world has been. God has given directions about our finances, but we haven't been paying attention and have been laying there paralyzed.

> *"But thou shalt remember the LORD thy God: for it is he that <u>giveth thee power to get wealth</u>, that he may establish his covenant which he sware unto thy fathers, as it is this day."*
> Deuteronomy 8:18

It is God who gives us the power to get wealth. He gives us the ability. He gives us the strength. He gives us the blessing. He gives us the wisdom. We are the ones who do the getting. God provides us with all the tools and ability we need, but we are the ones who have to use them to get the wealth He wants us to have.

Adam and Eve Worked in the Garden

> *"And God blessed them, and God said unto them, Be fruitful, and multiply, and replenish the earth, and subdue it: and <u>have dominion</u> over the fish of the sea, and over the fowl of the air, and over every living thing that moveth upon the earth. And God said, Behold, I have given you every herb bearing seed, which is upon the face of all the earth, and every tree, in the which is the fruit of a tree yielding seed; to you it shall be for meat."*
> Genesis 1:28-29

God Has Always Provided Wealth for His People

God created a world of abundance and gave it to Adam and Eve in the Garden. Notice God wasn't going to take care of the Garden for them. He wasn't going to do the work. He told THEM to take dominion over everything. It was their job to take care of the world He provided. They had a wonderful existence with beauty all around them. It was up to them to keep it that way. When Satan came into the Garden in chapter three of Genesis, God didn't do anything about it. He had given them responsibility for the Garden. It was their job to deal with this invader.

They should have taken dominion over Satan and kicked his butt right out of the Garden as soon as he showed his face there. Instead of taking dominion over Satan like they should have, they sided with him and listened to him. They disobeyed God and brought sin into the world. And with sin came death and a curse on the earth.

> *"And unto Adam he said, Because thou hast hearkened unto the voice of thy wife, and hast eaten of the tree, of which I commanded thee, saying, Thou shalt not eat of it: cursed is the ground for thy sake; in sorrow shalt thou eat of it all the days of thy life; Thorns also and thistles shall it bring forth to thee; and thou shalt eat the herb of the field;"*
> Genesis 3:17-18

The ground became cursed at this point and weeds started growing. So, all the farmers and gardeners out there have Adam to thank for those weeds. Up until this time Adam and Eve simply worked under a blessing. Now they would work under a curse for the rest of their lives. God forced them out of the Garden of Eden for their disobedience. They survived, but had to work the rest of their lives for a much smaller return. They no longer lived in the beauty of Eden. They no longer tended a Garden without weeds. From now on, they just went into survival mode without the blessing of God on their work.

The whole world is still working under a curse to this day. The highest rate of heart attacks occurs on Monday morning when people return to work each week. Hard work doesn't kill you, but stress can destroy your body in just a few years. People are stressed about work, about layoffs, and about how they will take care of their families. It is all the result of the original sin by Adam in the Garden.

God Makes a Covenant for Real Estate

Man and God were separated by sin. They could no longer be in fellowship, and man suffered because of it. God waited until He could find a man who would believe Him and be willing to make a Covenant with Him.

> *"Now the LORD had said unto Abram, Get thee out of thy country, and from thy kindred, and from thy father's house, unto a land that I will shew thee: And I will make of thee a great nation, and I will bless thee, and make thy name great; and thou shalt be a blessing:"*
> Genesis 12:1-2

This is the first statement God made to Abraham. God basically promised him four things in this first contact:

1. He would produce a great nation out of Abraham.
2. He would bless Abraham.
3. He would make Abraham's name great.
4. Abraham would become a blessing to others.

What is a result of God's blessing on Abraham? We can see a portion of the promises above come to pass almost immediately. A famine occurs in the land and Abraham travels down to Egypt. Look what it says about him in Genesis chapter thirteen when he leaves Egypt.

*"And Abram went up out of Egypt, he, and his wife, and all that he had, and Lot with him, into the south. And Abram was **very rich** in cattle, in silver, and in gold."*
Genesis 13:1-2

Notice that Abraham was not just rich when he left Egypt. He was very rich. The blessing was already occurring on Abraham before God even made the covenant with him. It was occurring because God said He would bless Him. It came because of God's word to Abraham. Let's fast forward over to when God officially makes a covenant with Abraham. This takes place in Genesis chapter fifteen:

"And he brought him forth abroad, and said, Look now toward heaven, and tell the stars, if thou be able to number them: and he said unto him, So shall thy seed be. And <u>he believed</u> in the LORD; and he counted it to him for righteousness. And he said unto him, I am the LORD that brought thee out of Ur of the Chaldees, to give thee this land to inherit it. And he said, Lord GOD, <u>whereby shall I know that I shall inherit it?</u> And he said unto him, Take me an heifer of three years old, and a she goat of three years old, and a ram of three years old, and a turtledove, and a young pigeon."
Genesis 15:5-9

Let's go over this in order. God promises Abraham his children would be like the stars of the sky so he could not even number them. Abraham BELIEVES the Lord and it is accounted to him for righteousness. So Abraham believes that part. He believes his children would be like the stars of the sky. What does Abraham have trouble believing? He has trouble believing God will give him the land to inherit. He basically tells God he can't believe it. So God makes a covenant with him for the land. Look at verse 18 in the same chapter.

> *"In the same day the LORD made a covenant with Abram, saying, Unto thy seed <u>have I given this land</u>, from the river of Egypt unto the great river, the river Euphrates:"*
> Genesis 15:18

The Lord made a covenant with Abraham for the land. This first covenant with Abraham was for real estate. Abraham had trouble believing God was going to give him all that real estate. The only way God could prove it to him was by making an unbreakable covenant promising Abraham the land.

It sounds like a lot of Christians today. They can believe in heaven. They can believe in salvation. They can believe in healing. They can believe in peace of mind. They can even believe in financial miracles. They just can't seem to bring themselves to believe in living in God's financial blessings everyday of their lives. They can't seem to believe God wants them to run their own business. They get upset if you tell them it's God will for them to own millions in real estate.

Isaac Became Wealthy Even in a Famine

God's financial blessings continued on in Abraham's family through his son Isaac. Isaac followed in his father's footsteps and the blessings of God made Isaac wealthy just like He did with Abraham. Let's go to Genesis chapter twenty-six when God talks specifically about why Isaac became wealthy.

> *"And there was <u>a famine in the land</u>, beside the first famine that was in the days of Abraham. And Isaac went unto Abimelech king of the Philistines unto Gerar. And the LORD appeared unto him, and said, Go not down into Egypt; <u>dwell in the land which I shall tell thee of</u>: Sojourn in this land, and I will be with thee, and will bless thee; for unto thee, and unto thy seed, I will give all these countries, and I will perform the oath which I sware unto Abraham thy father;"*

Genesis 26:1-3

A famine occurred in the land. God makes sure to let us know it was a different famine from the one Abraham experienced. It may have been as much as hundred years later. When a famine occurred in Abraham's time, he traveled down to Egypt. So Isaac was planning on following this same course of action. He was going to travel to Egypt to wait out the famine. God spoke to him and gave him wisdom by telling him where he should live during the famine (wisdom in this case was knowing exactly where to live to profit during the famine). So God gave him direction about where he should live to be most profitable.

> *"Then Isaac sowed in that land, <u>and received in the same year an hundredfold</u>: and the LORD blessed him. And the man waxed great, and went forward, and grew until he became very great: For he had possession of flocks, and possessions of herds, and great store of servants: and the Philistines envied him. For **all the wells** which his father's servants had digged in the days of Abraham his father, the Philistines had stopped them, and filled them with earth. And Abimelech said unto Isaac, Go from us; for thou art much mightier than we."*
> Genesis 26:12-16

Isaac went to the land the Lord sent him to, and he began farming. In the middle of a famine when no one else could grow crops, Isaac received hundredfold on what he planted. The Lord blessed him. How could Isaac's crops grow and return a maximum harvest when everyone else's was being destroyed by famine? Take notice the land he was farming in was full of wells. They must have produced the water needed to grow Isaac's crops during this time period...and to supply his flocks, his herds, and his servants.

God provided him with direction of where he should go and live during this period so he could profit in the time of famine. While everyone else was going broke, Isaac received specific wisdom from God so he could prosper and become greatly wealthy. When a recession or a depression comes, don't decide to participate. Go to God in prayer and ask him for wisdom of what you should do. He can give you directions that will make you wealthy just like He did for Isaac. God is no respecter of persons. What He did for one person, he will do for anyone who comes to Him with an open heart full of faith.

Isaac became so wealthy during this period that everyone around him became envious. They stopped up his wells and even ordered him to leave their area. They didn't want him around any longer because his wealth scared them.

God Made Jacob Wealthy Supernaturally

Jacob and Esau were born to Isaac and Rebekah. Jacob was deceitful and tricked Esau out of both his birthright and his blessing from Isaac. Because of his actions, Esau hated him and Jacob had to flee from his home to live with his uncle Laban.

While there, Jacob fell in love with Laban's daughter Rachel. He agreed to work for Laban for seven years to receive Rachel's hand in marriage. Laban deceived him though and gave his older daughter Leah to him in marriage. Jacob was forced to work another seven years to receive Rachel as his wife. He prepared to leave Laban with his wives after his fourteen years of service were finished. Laban asked him to continue to work for him because of the blessing of God he was receiving through Jacob's presence.

> *"And Laban said unto him, I pray thee, if I have found favour in thine eyes, tarry: for I have learned by experience that <u>the LORD hath blessed me for thy sake.</u>"*
> Genesis 30:27

The blessing of God was upon Jacob. Laban, his employer, was blessed just for Jacob's sake. Keep that in mind in your own life. Your employer and people you work with may

God Has Always Provided Wealth for His People

be blessed just because of you! That's how important the blessing of God is on your life and those around you.

Laban and Jacob agree to a deal for Jacob to be paid in cattle and sheep for him to continue to work. They make a deal that Jacob will receive all the speckled and spotted animals, the black sheep, and the spotted and speckled goats for his wages. Laban acts deceitfully again and tries to rip Jacob off…

> *"I will pass through all thy flock to day, removing from thence all the speckled and spotted cattle, and all the brown cattle among the sheep, and the spotted and speckled among the goats: and of such shall be my hire. So shall my righteousness answer for me in time to come, when it shall come for my hire before thy face: every one that is not speckled and spotted among the goats, and brown among the sheep, that shall be counted stolen with me. And Laban said, Behold, I would it might be according to thy word. <u>And he removed that day</u> the he goats that were ringstraked and spotted, and all the she goats that were speckled and spotted, and every one that had some white in it, and all the brown among the sheep, and gave them into the hand of his sons. And he set three days' journey betwixt himself and Jacob: and Jacob fed the rest of Laban's flocks."*
>
> Genesis 30:32-36

Jacob and Laban agree that Jacob will get all the speckled and spotted animals, black sheep, and speckled and spotted goats. Laban then quickly removes ALL of those types of animals from his herds. He takes them and moves them 3 days journey away from the herds Jacob will be watching. Under these conditions, it should be impossible for Jacob to earn anything for his work.

> *"And Jacob took him rods of green poplar, and of the hazel and chesnut tree; and pilled white strakes in them, and made the white appear which was in the rods. And*

he set the rods which he had pilled before the flocks in the gutters in the watering troughs when the flocks came to drink, that they should conceive when they came to drink. And the flocks conceived before the rods, and brought forth cattle ringstraked, speckled, and spotted. And Jacob did separate the lambs, and set the faces of the flocks toward the ringstraked, and all the brown in the flock of Laban; and he put his own flocks by themselves, and put them not unto Laban's cattle. And it came to pass, whensoever the stronger cattle did conceive, that Jacob laid the rods before the eyes of the cattle in the gutters, that they might conceive among the rods. But when the cattle were feeble, he put them not in: so the feebler were Laban's, and the stronger Jacob's. And the <u>man increased exceedingly, and had much cattle, and maidservants, and menservants, and camels, and asses.</u>"
Genesis 30:37-43

This is a supernatural miracle by God to make Jacob wealthy. With the odds stacked completely against Jacob and all of his future pay completely removed from the flock, ALL of the stronger cattle end up becoming spotted and speckled. He ended up getting all the best of Laban's herds as his own through God's supernatural intervention. No matter what Laban tried to do to deceive and rob Jacob, God turned it around. The blessing of God made Jacob rich in spite of his employer working against him and treating him unfairly.

Your employer is not your source. God is your source. Even if your employer is out to get you just like Laban's was, God can still bless you and prosper you in that situation. You may work for a company where your boss or other people take credit for your work. They may get a promotion for something you have done. Don't allow yourself to get bitter in those circumstances.

You don't work for them. You work for the Lord and are doing your job as unto the Lord. He is your source and He will see to it that you receive His blessing on your work. You can prosper and become wealthy irregardless of whom you currently work for if you keep seeking God's kingdom first in your life.

Joseph's Gifts Promote Him

The youngest child of Jacob was Joseph, and he had a special gift from God. God gave him dreams and the ability to interpret those dreams. This special ability would eventually take Joseph from the prison to the palace. In the meantime, his gifting would cause hatred among his brethren.

> *"And when his brethren saw that their father loved him more than all his brethren, <u>they hated him</u>, and could not speak peaceably unto him. And Joseph dreamed a dream, and he told it his brethren: and they hated him yet the more."*
> Genesis 37:4-5

His brother's hatred of him eventually caused them to throw him into a pit and then sell him as a slave to traveling merchants. The merchants were traveling on their way to Egypt and sold Joseph to Potiphar, one of the officers of the Pharaoh. There Joseph worked as a slave and God prospered him in spite of his circumstances.

> *"And the LORD was with Joseph, and he was a prosperous man; and he was in the house of his master the Egyptian. And his master saw that the LORD was with him, and that the LORD made <u>all that he did to prosper in his hand</u>. And Joseph found grace in his sight, and he served him: and he made him overseer over his house, and all that he had he put into his hand. And it came to pass from the time that he had made him overseer in his house, and over all that he had, that the LORD blessed the Egyptian's house for Joseph's sake;*

and the blessing of the LORD was upon all that he had in the house, and in the field."
Genesis 39:2-5

Joseph was so well liked and so prosperous in the house of Potiphar that he was in control of all the finances of the house. Potiphar didn't even know what he owned anymore as everything in the house was controlled by Joseph. Even in slavery, the blessing of God caused Joseph to be prosperous and receive divine favor from others.

The only problem was that he got a little too much favor and the wife of Potiphar began trying to seduce him to sleep with her. He refused because of his integrity before God and Potiphar. She eventually accused him of rape for resisting her advances and had him thrown into prison.

"And it came to pass, when his master heard the words of his wife, which she spake unto him, saying, After this manner did thy servant to me; that his wrath was kindled. And Joseph's master took him, and put him into the prison, a place where the king's prisoners were bound: and he was there in the prison. But the LORD was with Joseph, and shewed him mercy, and <u>gave him favour</u> in the sight of the keeper of the prison. And the keeper of the prison committed to Joseph's hand all the prisoners that were in the prison; and whatsoever they did there, he was the doer of it. The keeper of the prison looked not to any thing that was under his hand; because the LORD was with him, and that which he did, <u>the LORD made it to prosper</u>."
Genesis 39:19-23

This is the second time in his life he was stabbed in the back by someone close by. First his brothers sold him into slavery. Now the wife of his trusted master accuses him of a crime he didn't commit. By most people's standards Joseph would have every right to have a pity-party now. He gets ahead in life only to be robbed by a deceitful vindictive woman.

Does Joseph give up and quit? No. He doesn't. He continues to do his job as unto the Lord. The Lord blesses him with favor with the keeper of the prison. The same success Joseph had in Potiphar's house was then produced inside of the prison. The Lord made everything Joseph did to prosper. He was put in charge of the prison and managed everything that went on in there.

Both the chief butler and the chief baker were sent to prison at the time Joseph was managing it. They both received dreams and needed someone to interpret them. Joseph interpreted both the dreams. The chief butler's dream meant that he would be back serving the Pharaoh in 3 days. The chief baker's dream meant he would be beheaded within 3 days time. The baker was hanged and the butler was restored to his position just as Joseph said would happen. The butler forgot all about Joseph for the next two years.

After two years, the Pharaoh had a dream that none of his wise men or magicians could interpret. The chief butler finally remembered Joseph and told Pharaoh about his experiences with him in prison. Joseph was called immediately and asked to interpret the dream for Pharaoh.

"And Joseph said unto Pharaoh, The dream of Pharaoh is one: God hath shewed Pharaoh what he is about to do. The seven good kine are seven years; and the seven good ears are seven years: the dream is one. And the seven thin and ill favoured kine that came up after them are seven years; and the seven empty ears blasted with the east wind shall be seven years of famine. This is the thing which I have spoken unto Pharaoh: What God is about to do he sheweth unto Pharaoh. Behold, there come seven years of great plenty throughout all the land of Egypt: And there shall arise after them seven years of famine; and all the plenty shall be forgotten in the land of Egypt; and the famine shall consume the land; And

> *the plenty shall not be known in the land by reason of that famine following; for it shall be very grievous. And for that the dream was doubled unto Pharaoh twice; it is because the thing is established by God, and God will shortly bring it to pass. Now therefore let Pharaoh look out a man discreet and wise, and set him over the land of Egypt. Let Pharaoh do this, and let him appoint officers over the land, and take up the fifth part of the land of Egypt in the seven plenteous years. And let them gather all the food of those good years that come, and lay up corn under the hand of Pharaoh, and let them keep food in the cities. And that food shall be for store to the land against the seven years of famine, which shall be in the land of Egypt; that the land perish not through the famine."*
> Genesis 41:25-36

The dreams Pharaoh received were from God telling him there would soon be seven years of great harvests. They would be prosperous years for everyone. After those years would come seven years of famine in which no one would be able to grow crops. The seven years of famine would be enough to destroy the land if something wasn't done about it during the seven prosperous years.

> *"And Pharaoh said unto his servants, Can we find such a one as this is, a man in whom the Spirit of God is? And Pharaoh said unto Joseph, Forasmuch as God hath shewed thee all this, there is none so discreet and wise as thou art: Thou shalt be over my house, and according unto thy word shall all my people be ruled: <u>only in the throne will I be greater than thou</u>. And Pharaoh said unto Joseph, See, I have set thee over all the land of Egypt. And Pharaoh took off his ring from his hand, and put it upon Joseph's hand, and arrayed him in vestures of fine linen, and put a gold chain about his neck; And he made him to ride in the second chariot which he had;*

and they cried before him, Bow the knee: and he made him ruler over all the land of Egypt."
Genesis 41:38-43

Joseph was immediately promoted to second in charge of Egypt. He would manage all of Egypt and would take care of all the plans for managing the harvests. Egypt and the lives of all the surrounding people were saved by God's wisdom and Joseph's management of the country.

"And all countries came into Egypt to Joseph for to buy corn; because that the famine was so sore in all lands."
Genesis 41:57

Egypt became even more prosperous than they already were because all the nations came to purchase corn from them. They were the only country to have received the plan and to have prepared for the famine. So they succeeded during famine through the wisdom of God in Joseph. Even his brethren came to purchase food during this time and bowed their knees to him as the leader of Egypt.

The dream he had as young man came to pass in his life. It took many years and he went through quite a few setbacks. Many people would have simply given up and gotten bitter at God and people if they went through the same experiences Joseph went through. Instead, Joseph looked at each setback as a new opportunity in his life.

Failures Look at Setbacks as Opportunities to Give Up. Champions look at Setbacks as a Set-Up for their Next Step Up.

First Joseph learned how to manage a large household while working as a slave for Potiphar. Then he was sent to prison and it looked like a demotion. Instead, in this place he received God's favor and blessing again, and he learned how to manage something much larger in running the entire prison. So he had experience in managing both a large household and the prison system before he was promoted to running all of Egypt.

If Joseph wouldn't have been put in those places of authority earlier on in his life, he would have never had the wisdom he would have needed to manage Egypt. Having the knowledge that 7 years of plenteousness and 7 years of famine were coming were one thing. Knowing what to do about it and how to manage the whole process is something quite a bit different.

God wants to give you big visions and dreams for your life, but you may not be ready for them for years to come. On the way there you will encounter opposition. You will encounter jealous people who try to make you fail. You will have opportunities to give up or get bitter at people just like Joseph did.

The question is, "How will you react?" Will you look at setbacks as opportunities to give up and quit? Will you quit playing the game and quit on your dreams? Will you become the kind of person who holds others back because you refuse to push through to your success?

Or will you be like Joseph? Will you look at the setbacks and use them as the set-up for your next step-up in life? If you are laid off from your job, rejoice. Pray to God for wisdom in finding an even better job. If your boss demotes you to a lower position for no good reason, find a way to succeed at this new job and get yourself promoted back above your boss.

Every step in Joseph's life was used to teach him another level of management. He managed a house. He managed a prison. Then he managed Egypt. Every job you take should become a learning experience for your next step in life.

You may be working at McDonald's today. You may be cooking burgers. Well, set your mind to become the best burger cook there and do the best job that can possibly be done. Make an effort to learn everything you can at this job. When you're promoted, keep learning everything you can about managing the people who work there. When you're promoted again, learn everything you can there. God's plan for your life may be for you to own 15 McDonald's in the future and everything you learn today will be used to make them as successful as possible in the future.

No matter where you are today you can begin your learning experience for the next step up in your life. You will not reach your dreams and visions overnight, but every day is another step closer if you keep learning and reaching for them.

You are not working for man in your job. You are working for God. He is the one who notices you, blesses you, and promotes you. Whenever you start to forget that, spend some time reading through Genesis thirty-seven to fifty.

Chapter Three
The Wealth of the Wicked is Laid Up for the Righteous

> *"And the children of Israel were fruitful, and increased abundantly, and multiplied, and <u>waxed exceeding mighty</u>; and the land was filled with them. Now there arose up a new king over Egypt, which knew not Joseph. And he said unto his people, Behold, the people of the children of Israel are more and mightier than we: Come on, let us deal wisely with them; lest they multiply, and it come to pass, that, when there falleth out any war, they join also unto our enemies, and fight against us, and so get them up out of the land. Therefore they did set over them taskmasters to afflict them with their burdens. And they built for Pharaoh treasure cities, Pithom and Raamses. But <u>the more they afflicted them, the more they multiplied and grew</u>. And they were grieved because of the children of Israel."*
> Exodus 1:7-12

The people of Israel lived in Egypt and were satisfied for hundreds of years. There were only 70 people in Jacob's family total when they first came to Egypt because of the famine. They continued to multiply and grow in number during the period until there were over a million of them at this point in history.

There were so many of the children of Israel that when a new king arose over Egypt he was terrified of them. He was afraid they may band together with any of Egypt's enemies and destroy them. This new king didn't remember how Joseph had saved his country and his people hundreds of years ago. So he set out to break their spirits and turned them into slaves to build his cities.

The goal of the slavery and the harsh treatment that began for the children of the Israel was to break their spirits, destroy their health, and keep them from multiplying. They accomplished the goal of destroying their spirits which we will find out about later as we go deeper into this study. They were not able to destroy their health or to keep them from multiplying. Even in the bondage, the children of Israel continued to multiply and grow.

So the king of Egypt went even further and began killing all of the boys born to the Hebrews. His goal was to completely destroy their strength and getting rid of all their sons was his final plan for accomplishing this. This was the kind of situation Moses was born into. When he was three months old, his mother hid him inside of a wicker basket in the Nile River.

The daughter of Pharaoh found him and claimed him as her own. She hired the original mother to nurse Moses for her. So Moses' mother ended up being paid a salary to take care of her own son. When Moses grew old enough, he was taken in as the child of Pharaoh's daughter.

> *"And when he was cast out, Pharaoh's daughter took him up, and nourished him for her own son. And Moses was <u>learned in all the wisdom of the Egyptians</u>, and was <u>mighty in words and in deeds</u>. And when he was full forty years old, it came into his heart to visit his brethren the children of Israel."*
> Acts 7:21-23

Moses was raised and taught in all the wisdom of the Egyptians. He would have had the best education available in the world at the time as the Egyptians were a very advanced people. He would have also been taught all about their government and how it operated. This would have all in been in preparation for God's calling him to be the leader of the children of Israel and for his eventual contact with Pharaoh during their deliverance.

The Jewish historian Josephus also reports that during this training Moses also became a general in the Egyptian army where he led a war against the Aethiopians. So Moses became mighty in both words (being trained in all the knowledge of the Egyptians) and in deeds (being a general and mighty leader).

He was trained for forty years in words and deeds until the day he decided to visit the children of Israel. He was moved in his heart to visit his own people. When he saw one of them being oppressed and beaten, he couldn't stand for it. He took action and killed the Egyptian. He thought the Hebrew would be grateful for his actions and that they would understand he was sent for their deliverance, but they didn't understand it.

> *"For <u>he supposed his brethren would have understood how that God by his hand would deliver them: but they understood not</u>. And the next day he shewed himself unto them as they strove, and would have set them at one again, saying, Sirs, ye are brethren; why do ye wrong one to another? But he that did his neighbour wrong thrust him away, saying, Who made thee a ruler and a judge over us? Wilt thou kill me, as thou diddest the Egyptian yesterday? Then fled Moses at this saying, and was a stranger in the land of Madian, where he begat two sons."*
> Acts 7:25-29

There was no one else there except Moses, the Egyptian, and the Hebrew he saved. The Egyptian was killed so he obviously didn't tell anyone. Moses didn't tell anyone about it either. So the Hebrew is the one that told everybody about what Moses did.

The Pharaoh wanted to kill him for his actions and the people of Israel rejected him. So Moses fled the country to hide out in the desert. The people he had been sent to save rejected their deliverance by asking him, "Who made you a ruler and judge over us?" They didn't believe in his calling, and Moses went into hiding from both his calling and his country.

God met Moses on the backside of the desert in a burning bush. He spoke to Moses out of the burning bush and told him he was going back to Egypt to free his people from their bondage. The 40 year old hurt and rejection Moses had felt when he left Egypt was still in him and he couldn't believe the message from God.

> *"Come now therefore, and I will send thee unto Pharaoh, that thou mayest bring forth my people the children of Israel out of Egypt. And Moses said unto God, <u>Who am I, that I should go unto Pharaoh</u>, and that I should bring forth the children of Israel out of Egypt? And he said, Certainly I will be with thee; and this shall be a token unto thee, that I have sent thee: When thou hast brought forth the people out of Egypt, ye shall serve God upon this mountain. And Moses said unto God, Behold, when I come unto the children of Israel, and shall say unto them, The God of your fathers hath sent me unto you; and they shall say to me, What is his name? what shall I say unto them?"*
> Exodus 3:10-13

Moses no longer believes in his calling. When he was 40 years old he believed he was sent to deliver his people from their bondage. We can see that from the Scripture we read in Acts. He believed it so strongly he killed one of the Egyptians hurting his brethren. His brethren were the ones that didn't believe in his calling.

The Hebrews had rejected Moses out of their own pain and hurt. The years they spent in bondage drove them to not accept him for their deliverance. The emotional wounds he received from their rejection have by this time affected him and he no longer believes he is called to deliver them anymore either. It's been a long time and Moses just doesn't accept his calling even when God is speaking to him in person.

One of his first questions to God is how will he prove to the Israelites that God was the one sending him to deliver them. They didn't believe him the first time so he doesn't expect them to believe him this time either. Moses goes even further in revealing his true mindset in this next passage...

> *"And Moses said unto the LORD, O my Lord, <u>I am not eloquent, neither heretofore, nor since thou hast spoken unto thy servant</u>: but I am slow of speech, and of a slow tongue. And the LORD said unto him, Who hath made man's mouth? or who maketh the dumb, or deaf, or the seeing, or the blind? have not I the LORD? Now therefore go, and I will be with thy mouth, and teach thee what thou shalt say. And he said, O my Lord, send, I pray thee, by the hand of him whom thou wilt send. And the anger of the LORD was kindled against Moses, and he said, Is not Aaron the Levite thy brother? I know that he can speak well. And also, behold, he cometh forth to meet thee: and when he seeth thee, he will be glad in his heart. And thou shalt speak unto him, and put words in his mouth: and I will be with thy mouth, and with his mouth, and will teach you what ye shall do."*
> Exodus 4:10-15

Moses complains to God that he is not eloquent and that he is slow of speech and of tongue. He basically tells God he is not going to be able to do the job because he isn't a very good speaker. Yet Acts 7:22 says he was mighty in both words and deeds. So he obviously was very good with words. He lied to God because the 40 years he had spent in the wilderness made him forget who he really was.

The children of Israel had been in bondage to the Egyptians for so long that they forgot who they were...a powerful people prosperous and blessed of the Lord. Moses had been on the backside of the desert suffering rejection from both his adopted family the Egyptians and his true family the

Hebrews that he forgot who he was…a fully trained man in both mighty words and deeds.

The Lord became angry with Moses and had to have Aaron brought along to be Moses' mouthpiece. Most believers today never step into their full calling from God because of fear and pain from their past. They don't believe they can do it and they settle for something less than God's perfect will for their lives.

God sent Moses back into Egypt and there he demanded Pharaoh to let his people go. Pharaoh not only refused, but he decided to add additional work to the Hebrew slaves. He used to provide bricks for their daily work. Now he required them to make their own bricks and still finish the same amount of work each day. The situation went from bad to worse after Moses got involved on their behalf.

God continued to send Moses back to Pharaoh time and time again. Each time Pharaoh would harden his heart and refuse to allow the children of Israel to leave. Moses dropped his staff and it turned into a serpent. The Pharaoh's magicians did the same thing. God turned the waters of the Nile into blood…and the magicians did the same thing (don't ask me why they wanted even more bloody water). God sent frogs to cover the entire land. The magicians of Egypt decided to make some extra frogs to also cover their land (I guess they didn't think God punished them with enough frogs). Then God turned all the dust of Egypt into lice (the magicians tried to make some more lice, but they weren't able).

God continued to send plague after plague onto the land. He sent flies. He killed all the cattle of Egypt. He sent boils upon all the Egyptians. He sent hail onto the land that destroyed everyone and everything in the fields. He sent so many locusts that you weren't even able to see the ground through them. He sent a darkness that covered the whole land for three days. During this whole process Pharaoh agreed to let the children of Israel go multiple times. He would agree and God would remove the plaque. As soon as the plague left, he'd change his mind and keep them in bondage. The plagues continued one after another until the final one.

The final plague was to slay the firstborn son of every household in Egypt. The Israelites held a Passover feast and put blood on the doorposts that the death angel would not come through their house (symbolic of Jesus' blood covering and protecting us). Every firstborn in Egypt died that night and the Pharaoh finally let the people of Israel go. But they didn't go empty handed...

> *"And the children of Israel did according to the word of Moses; and they <u>borrowed</u> of the Egyptians jewels of silver, and jewels of gold, and raiment: And the LORD gave the people favour in the sight of the Egyptians, so that they lent unto them such things as they required. And <u>they spoiled the Egyptians</u>."*
> Exodus 12:35-36

Not only did the Israelites leave with all of their own belongings including their herds of cattle, but they also took all the silver, gold, and raiment of the Egyptians with them. I always wondered about that word "borrowed" in this passage. It makes it sound like they were planning on giving it back. The correct Hebrew word would be "sha'al" here and it really means, "to inquire, to request, to demand." They basically demanded the Egyptians give them their belongings to take with them!

After the Israelites left, Pharaoh's heart was again hardened and he chased after them with his armies. They followed the Israelites to the Red Sea where God performed the miracle of rolling back the water for the Israelites to walk on dry ground. The Egyptians were all killed when God allowed the water to roll back into place overtop them. This was all to fulfill the prophecy God had spoken to Abraham hundreds of years before...

> *"And also that nation, whom they shall serve, will I judge: and afterward shall they come out with <u>great substance</u>."*
> Genesis 15:14

No matter how much people would try to oppress the Israelites, they would come out on top. We have seen this time and time again all throughout their history. God's blessing on their lives would make them a success every time no matter what stood in their way.

> *"The blessing of the LORD, it maketh rich, and he addeth no sorrow with it."*
> Proverbs 10:22

God made Abraham very rich. He also made him a promise that his descendants would get the prime real estate in the area…something he almost couldn't believe until God made a covenant with him. Isaac followed in his father's footsteps and became wealthy right in the middle of a famine. While everyone else was going broke, Isaac was earning a fortune because of God's direction and His blessing.

Jacob became wealthy while working for a boss who constantly deceived him and kept trying to trick him. In fact, the Word says Laban changed Jacob's wages a total of 10 times while he was there. When everything was against him, God made him supernaturally wealthy by changing the very course of nature (making regular animals have unusual colors in their children).

Joseph was born with a gift. He had dreams and could interpret the dreams of others by God's help. This made his family jealous and they sold him into slavery. This couldn't stop him as his wisdom and God's divine favor took him to managing Potiphar's house. The wife lusted for him and accused him of a crime he didn't commit landing him in prison.

Instead of getting bitter, he simply continued working hard, walking in God's blessing and receiving favor in prison.

He soon managed the whole prison. When the day came for his gift to shine, he had already proven himself faithful continually. He interpreted Pharaoh's dream and was put in charge over all of Egypt. All of his previous experiences in management were put to the test as the whole world was saved through his wisdom.

A Pharaoh took over that didn't know Joseph and he put the Israelites into bondage and slavery. They cried out to God to deliver them and He brought up Moses. Moses received all the education Egypt could provide. He became both trained in speech and also in military leadership. He was thoroughly prepared for the day he would lead the million plus Israelites out of their bondage.

When the Hebrews first rejected him at coming to the aid of one of them, he fled the country to hide in the desert. The rejection he felt held him so far back that when God came to him 40 years later he told God he couldn't even speak (after receiving all the Egyptian training in it). His self-esteem had been completely destroyed. God used him in spite of this and he led the Israelites out of their bondage along with all the wealth of Egypt.

No matter what obstacles they faced or who were against them, with the blessing of God His people always came out on top. The blessing of God makes rich, and He adds no sorrow to it. We could continue to cover story after story in the Old Testament about God's blessing to make His people wealthy, but the ones we have covered should be enough to prove to you it is God's desire to bless you financially. Remember, God is no respecter of persons. What He did for one, He will do for all who come to Him in faith.

Solomon's wealth is one of the greatest examples in all of history about God's desire to bless His people financially. He prayed to God for wisdom instead of money, and God blessed him with unbelievable amounts of both. Proverbs is one of our greatest examples of Solomon's wisdom. The statement the queen of Sheba said about Solomon is one of the best to show his incredible wealth...

"And when the queen of Sheba had seen all Solomon's wisdom, and the house that he had built, And the meat of his table, and the sitting of his servants, and the attendance of his ministers, and their apparel, and his cupbearers, and his ascent by which he went up unto the house of the LORD; <u>there was no more spirit in her</u>. And she said to the king, It was a true report that I heard in mine own land of thy acts and of thy wisdom. Howbeit I believed not the words, until I came, and mine eyes had seen it: and, behold, the half was not told me<u>: thy wisdom and prosperity exceedeth the fame</u> which I heard."
1 Kings 10:4-7

Solomon's wisdom and prosperity exceeded the fame of what everyone had been told. If you're like me, you've seen advertisements and heard a lot of stories. Once you actually get a hold of the product being sold or see something with your own eyes, it ends up being a disappointment. It rarely ever comes anywhere near as exciting as the ad makes it sound. In Solomon's case, the queen of Sheba said everything she saw exceeded all the reports she heard about it. A queen of another wealthy land was amazed at Israel's wealth and prosperity.

It all came because of one simple prayer Solomon made to God for wisdom...the same type of prayer He has told you to pray in James chapter one.

What About Job?

Anytime you start teaching about God's desire to bless His people and about His promises, someone always seems to bring up Job. They feel God's promises don't apply to them, because they feel they are like "Poor Old Job." They always talk about the trials they're going through and how God must be trying to teach them something. Their situation in life never gets any better and they sure don't ever learn anything. They believe God just must be trying to keep them humble in those circumstances.

They may be bound by poverty and getting deeper in debt every month. Every new job they get, they might lose in only a month's time. It may be that they can never find a new job. No matter what the problem is…they see it and claim it is God putting them through a trial to teach them something. The example they always use to try to prove their case is "Poor Old Job." They talk about how he lost everything and experienced those horrible boils. I've even heard some people use a statement, "As poor as Job's turkeys." They think they're just a modern day example of Job's suffering.

There is a major problem with their whole belief system. Job was a very rich man. His trials recorded in the book of Job only lasted around 9 months total. At the end of the trial, he became twice as wealthy as he was in the beginning.

> "His substance also was seven thousand sheep, and three thousand camels, and five hundred yoke of oxen, and five hundred she asses, and a very great household; so that this man was the <u>greatest of all the men of the east</u>."
> Job 1:3

> "So the LORD blessed the latter end of Job more than his beginning: for he had fourteen thousand sheep, and six thousand camels, and a thousand yoke of oxen, and a thousand she asses."
> Job 42:12

We don't have a record of how long Job lived before his trial, but we do know that Job lived another 140 years after it. For a man who must have lived hundreds of years, he was only poor for 9 months total. Since our lifespans are only a limited amount of what his was, this would equal less than 3 months of our own life spans. So anyone who says they are like "Poor Old Job" must mean they were one of the richest people in the US. They had some kind of financial problems and have went bankrupt for around 3 months or so. As soon as their bankruptcy is up, they plan on becoming even wealthier than they were in the beginning.

Job's financial situation could be compared to what has happened many times in the last few decades. You'll hear about a major millionaire on TV having to declare bankruptcy. Their business all of sudden hit a huge dip or all their real estate holdings lost value for some reason. They have to declare bankruptcy. A few months later you turn on the news and you hear about how they are doing multi-million dollar deals again. They've regained their millionaire status in just a few months. They were able to do the things that made them wealthy in the first place much quicker this time because they already had knowledge and experience.

It has often been said that if we redistributed all the wealth on this planet equally to everyone we would all receive around a million each. Wait five years, and the same people who have the money today would again have the majority of the money in their accounts. It is their wisdom which takes and multiplies the money.

Let's take a step back and look at the other problem most people experience when they read through the book of Job. They see the things Job says throughout the book and they begin quoting them for their own doctrine or their own life. The mistake they're making is they do not understand where all those discussions ended. When God appears in Job chapter thirty-eight and on, He rebukes Job and his three friends for all the statements they make throughout the entire book. The whole book of Job shows us all the WRONG beliefs people have about God through Job and his friends.

Yet, many people in our day are latching onto some of these statements and making some very ridiculous statements about how God operates. They say things like, "The Lord giveth, and the Lord taketh away, blessed be the name of the Lord." It's obvious throughout the book Satan is the one who "taketh away." Yet, they still make those statements. They are simply setting themselves up to be rebuked by God just as Job was.

What was Job's response once God appears and rebukes him?

> *"I have heard of thee by the hearing of the ear: but now mine eye seeth thee. Wherefore I abhor myself, and repent in dust and ashes."*
> Job 42:5-6

Job is the oldest book of the Bible. Most likely he lived around the same time as Abraham. So there was no covenant with God at his time. He did not have a covenant with God like we do. He had never heard from God directly. He did not have any written recordings of how God operates like we have (the entire Bible is a recording of the way God operates). His only knowledge of God is what he had heard from other people. This is what you see him quoting throughout the book of Job. He is quoting and making statements He and his friends have heard others say falsely about God. Once he sees the real God with his own eyes, he repents in dust and ashes for the statements he has made.

With God having given you 66 books recording exactly how He operates, his complete dealings with dozens of his servants, and His everlasting covenant with you personally through Jesus…what is your excuse? So next time you hear someone talk about "Poor Old Job," you should have a completely different reaction. Great! They're wealthy…are having some short-term problems and trials…and will soon breakthrough to even greater success than ever before.

Remember what we learned from Joseph…

Failures Look at Setbacks as Opportunities to Give Up. Champions look at Setbacks as a Set-Up for their Next Step Up.

Chapter Four
Was Jesus Poor?

The church is often full of religious traditions that have no basis in reality whatsoever. For example, many preachers will try to convince you Jesus was poor throughout his earthly ministry. They take verses out of context to do this and completely ignore all the ones about the material prosperity surrounding Jesus. A belief such as this can severely limit your thinking about God's blessings. If God allowed His own Son Jesus to live in lack, then you would forever have doubts about God blessing you financially.

We're going to spend a little time in the Word to show you that not only was Jesus not poor, but money was actually following and hunting him down. First let's cover a couple of myths some preachers have portrayed about Jesus. The first one is that some people are saying Jesus was born in a manger in a stable because his parents were poor. This is definitely not true. Let's take a look at what the Word says about his birth.

> *"And she brought forth her firstborn son, and wrapped him in swaddling clothes, and laid him in a manger; <u>because there was no room for them in the inn.</u>"*
> Luke 2:7

Some people may have read that verse and thought it said because they could not afford the inn. That is not what is says. It says, "Because there was no room for them at the inn." So obviously Joseph and Mary first went to the inn to get a room (or how else would they know there was no room for them).

Joseph and Mary had to travel to Bethlehem to pay their taxes and when they got there they found that all the inns were already sold out to other people paying their taxes. So it had nothing to do with being able to afford a room. Not only were they looking for a room, but they were also there to pay their taxes (if you don't have money, you can't pay your taxes).

Another myth people sometimes fall into is believing Jesus was homeless. He says one time (recorded in two different Gospels) that he has nowhere to lay his head on one occasion. If you don't read other Bible verses, this can be taken out of context and used to try to portray Jesus as a homeless man just wondering around.

> *"And a certain scribe came, and said unto him, Master, I will follow thee whithersoever thou goest. And Jesus saith unto him, The foxes have holes, and the birds of the air have nests; but <u>the Son of man hath not where to lay his head</u>."*
> Matthew 8:19-20

Why did Jesus say he didn't have anywhere to lay his head? It's because he did not have an "enduring" home here on this earth. He was not of the earth. His true home is in heaven (just like your true home is in heaven if you're born again). He is not permanently accepted in any location while he was in his active ministry on this earth. His ministry was to travel around Israel preaching the Gospel and to eventually die at the cross for our sins.

Jesus' physical home was in Nazareth at first, and he later moved to Capernaum. This is shown in this Scripture...

> *"And leaving Nazareth, he came and <u>dwelt in Capernaum</u>, which is <u>upon the sea coast</u>, in the borders of Zabulon and Nephthalim:"*
> Matthew 4:13

> *"And again he entered into Capernaum, after some days; and it was noised that he was in the house."*
> Mark 2:1

> *"And he entered into a ship, and passed over, and <u>came into his own city</u>."*
> Matthew 9:1

He wanted to have his dwelling place in Capernaum. Having a house down by the sea coast is always nice. It also makes traveling much easier since one of the primary modes of transportation at the time is by boat. In this next verse Jesus actually brings some visitors home with him.

> *"Then Jesus turned, and saw them following, and saith unto them, What seek ye? They said unto him, Rabbi, (which is to say, being interpreted, Master,) where dwellest thou? He saith unto them, Come and see. <u>They came and saw where he dwelt, and abode with him that day</u>: for it was about the tenth hour."*
> John 1:38-39

Not only did he have a home, but Jesus took those disciples over to stay with him for the day. Here they asked him where he dwells. So he showed them his home. In Matthew chapter eight they asked him where he was going. So his reply was quite a bit different there as he had no final resting place on this earth.

Let's go to the final Scripture that some preachers try to use to portray a poor Jesus…

> *"For ye know the grace of our Lord Jesus Christ, that, <u>though he was rich</u>, yet for your sakes <u>he became poor</u>, that ye through his poverty might be rich."*
> 2 Corinthians 8:9

People read this Scripture and say that Jesus spent his life poor. What they fail to understand is this verse is one about the Substitutionary work Jesus provided for us at the cross. He was rich, and when he went to the cross he became poor for our sakes…that we may be made rich through him. We'll actually be covering this verse in the next chapter when you learn all about Jesus Substitutionary sacrifice.

He didn't go through his life poor. He went through his life prosperous. He became poor for us at the cross. To say he went through his life poor would be just as bad as saying he went through his life full of sin because he became sin at the cross for us also (II Cor 5:21). It was all a part of his Substitutionary work.

Jesus Walked in the Full Blessing of God Including Prosperity

Jesus fulfilled the law completely. Never once in his life did he fail or sin. He is the only person who has ever walked the earth perfect in every way. Up to his time, everyone had been put under the Law in the Old Testament to curb sin. But none of them kept the Law. They weren't able to keep the Law (read Romans 5 through 7 to fully understand this). Since Jesus was the fulfillment of the Law and kept it perfectly, let's see what the Word says about the blessings of keeping the Law...

> *"And it shall come to pass, if thou shalt hearken diligently unto the voice of the LORD thy God, to observe and to do all his commandments which I command thee this day, that the LORD thy God will set thee on high above all nations of the earth: And all these blessings shall come on thee, and overtake thee, if thou shalt hearken unto the voice of the LORD thy God. Blessed shalt thou be in the city, and blessed shalt thou be in the field. Blessed shall be the fruit of thy body, and the fruit of thy ground, and the fruit of thy cattle, the increase of thy kine, and the flocks of thy sheep. Blessed shall be thy basket and thy store. Blessed shalt thou be when thou comest in, and blessed shalt thou be when thou goest out. The LORD shall cause thine enemies that rise up against thee to be smitten before thy face: they shall come out against thee one way, and flee before thee seven ways.*

The LORD shall command the blessing upon thee in thy storehouses, and in all that thou settest thine hand unto; and he shall bless thee in the land which the LORD thy God giveth thee. The LORD shall establish thee an holy people unto himself, as he hath sworn unto thee, if thou shalt keep the commandments of the LORD thy God, and walk in his ways. And all people of the earth shall see that thou art called by the name of the LORD; and they shall be afraid of thee. And the LORD shall make thee plenteous in goods, in the fruit of thy body, and in the fruit of thy cattle, and in the fruit of thy ground, in the land which the LORD sware unto thy fathers to give thee. The LORD shall open unto thee his good treasure, the heaven to give the rain unto thy land in his season, and to bless all the work of thine hand: and thou shalt lend unto many nations, and thou shalt not borrow. And the LORD shall make thee the head, and not the tail; and thou shalt be above only, and thou shalt not be beneath; if that thou hearken unto the commandments of the LORD thy God, which I command thee this day, to observe and to do them: And thou shalt not go aside from any of the words which I command thee this day, to the right hand, or to the left, to go after other gods to serve them."
Deuteronomy 28:1-14

Let's count up and list all the blessings God tells us are received by keeping the Law. He says these blessings will come upon the obedient and that they will overtake them. So even if they are running away from them, the blessings will catch up to them and get them. They can't get away from God's blessings no matter where they go (if they're obedient).

1. You'd be blessed in the city.
2. You'd be blessed in the field.
3. The fruit of your body is blessed.
4. The fruit of your ground is blessed.

5. The fruit of your cattle is blessed.
6. Your kine will increase.
7. Your flock of sheep are blessed.
8. Your basket and store are blessed.
9. You're blessed when you come in.
10. You're blessed when you go out.
11. Your enemies will be smitten before your face.
12. Your enemies will flee before you in seven ways.
13. Your storehouses are blessed.
14. Everything you set your hand to do is blessed.
15. You'll be blessed in your land.
16. All the people will see you are God's and be afraid of you.
17. You will be plenteous in goods.
18. The fruit of your body will be plenteous.
19. The fruit of your cattle will be plenteous.
20. The fruit of your ground will be plenteous.
21. The Lord will give you good treasure.
22. You will receive rain when it is time.
23. All the work of your hand is blessed.
24. You will lend to many nations and not have to borrow.
25. You're the head and not the tail.
26. You are above and not beneath.

    This is just a quick listings of the blessings of keeping the Law from the above passage. If you keep reading through Deuteronomy 28 you will find many more blessings, and you will also find the curses of not keeping the Law. Since Jesus fulfilled the Law perfectly, then the blessing of prosperity from the Law had to be present in his life. Everything he put his hand to was prosperous. His basket was prosperous. His storehouses were prosperous. He was the head and not the tail (he always came out on top).

    Look at his birth for example. He was born in a manager because there was no room for him at the inn. As soon as he was born, money started chasing him down (all the blessings started overtaking him). Three wise men were looking for him at his birth bringing sacks of treasure.

> *"And when they were come into the house, they saw the young child with Mary his mother, and fell down, and worshipped him: and when they had <u>opened their treasures</u>, they presented unto him gifts; gold, and frankincense, and myrrh."*
> Matthew 2:11

The three wise men showed up with sacks of treasure. They gave him gold, frankincense, and myrrh...all extremely valuable. Jesus became wealthy and prosperous as soon as the wise men got there. And he stayed prosperous all the way until he laid it down for us at the cross.

Jesus Had His Own Treasurer & Often Gave to The Poor

> *"This he said, not that he cared for the poor; but because he was a thief, <u>and had the bag</u>, and bare what was put therein."*
> John 12:6

Judas was the treasurer for Jesus and the disciples. You don't need a treasurer if you don't have any money. You only need a treasurer if you have a lot of money coming in and going out. Somebody has to keep track of all the money going through their hands. This was Judas' job. On top of that, Judas was a thief. He would often help himself to what was put inside the bag. They always had enough money, constantly gave to the poor, and had a thief stealing the money at the same time.

There was obviously enough money in the bag that Judas could steal the money without anyone finding out about it. If you only have one dollar in your bag and someone steals it, that's pretty obvious. If you have a large amount of money in your bag, then it is much less likely to be found out. And none of the other disciples ever found out about him stealing from the bag (just think what hotheaded Peter's reaction would have been to that).

> *"For some of them thought, because Judas had the bag, that Jesus had said unto him, Buy those things that we have need of against the feast; or, that <u>he should give something to the poor</u>."*
> John 13:29

At the Passover feast, Judas left to betray Jesus to the Pharisees. All the other disciples at the Feast thought he was leaving either to buy things they needed for the feast or to give money to the poor. If they needed something for the feast, he could have been buying it since he had the bag. That is an obvious thought since they were having a feast together (and I'm sure the 13 of them needed quite a bit of food).

Why would they think Judas had left the meal to go give to the poor though? That's an unusual thought for the occasion. Normally people don't get up during a meal to leave and give money away. Why would they think about that? It must have been a common occurrence for Jesus to tell Judas to go give money to the poor in all types of occasions for them to think about this. It must have been a regular and everyday happening. They must have heard Jesus tell Judas to give money to poor people all the time.

Let's go to another instance in the life of Jesus that shows his attitude about money...

> *"So six days before the Passover Feast, Jesus came to Bethany, where Lazarus was, who had died and whom He had raised from the dead. So they made Him a supper; and Martha served, but Lazarus was one of those at the table with Him. Mary took a pound of ointment of pure liquid nard [a rare perfume] that was very expensive, and she poured it on Jesus' feet and wiped them with her hair. And the whole house was filled with*

the fragrance of the perfume. But Judas Iscariot, the one of His disciples who was about to betray Him, said, Why was this perfume not sold for 300 denarii [a year's wages for an ordinary workman] and that [money] given to the poor (the destitute)? Now he did not say this because he cared for the poor but because he was a thief; and having the bag (the money box, the purse of the Twelve), he took for himself what was put into it [pilfering the collections]. But Jesus said, Let her alone. It was [intended] that she should keep it for the time of My preparation for burial. [She has kept it that she might have it for the time of My embalming.] You always have the poor with you, but you do not always have Me."
John 12:1-8, AMP

Mary took very rare perfume and anointed the feet of Jesus with it. The price of this perfume if sold would have equaled a year's wages for an ordinary worker. That's a lot of money to pour on someone's feet. Jesus said she was acting correctly and that it had been saved for this very occasion, to anoint him for burial.

Judas is the one who got upset about this. He claimed she was wasting money that could have been given to the poor. Notice the mention of how important it was to give to the poor for them. In his own mind though, he wasn't thinking of it as being wasteful or of giving to the poor, he just wanted more money he could steal.

Poor people who weren't used to having anything wouldn't have been this relaxed about a year's salary being poured on someone's feet. Jesus wasn't upset about this at all. It was all part of the plan of God.

Jesus Had a Large Ministry With Many Partners

"After these things the Lord appointed other seventy also, and sent them two and two before his face into every city and place, whither he himself would come."

Luke 10:1

"And he said unto them, When I sent you without purse, and scrip, and shoes, lacked ye any thing? And they said, Nothing."
Luke 22:35

Jesus had 12 disciples and then these 70 also. Plus he had women, children, and other people who followed him around. That adds up to quite a large ministry. They traveled around the countryside by foot and by boat. Those people had to be fed. Those people had to be clothed. That is quite a group of ministers traveling around (and we all know how much ministers like to eat).

When Jesus asked them if they ever lacked anything (food, water, clothes, shelter), they responded "No." They never lacked anything during their travels. Everything they needed was provided for them. Finding 70 people who couldn't complain about any lack is quite an accomplishment (let's see you go to a local church of 70 or more and ask the same question).

Where did all the finances come to take care of all these people? Did they just miraculously appear out of the sky? Sure, there were times that Jesus multiplied food for everyone to eat and there was a time that Jesus sent Peter to get a gold piece out of a fish's mouth to pay his taxes. But the common everyday needs were taken care of by Jesus' ministry partners.

"And it came to pass afterward, that he went throughout every city and village, preaching and shewing the glad tidings of the kingdom of God: and the twelve were with him, And certain women, which had been healed of evil spirits and infirmities, Mary called Magdalene, out of whom went seven devils, And Joanna the wife of Chuza Herod's steward, and Susanna, and <u>many others</u>, which <u>ministered unto him of their substance</u>."
Luke 8:1-3

> *"Even so hath the Lord ordained that they which preach the gospel should live of the gospel."*
> 1 Corinthians 9:14

Mary, Joanna, Susanna, and many others ministered to him from their financial substance. They supplied the finances that were needed for the large group of people traveling around the countryside ministering. They can be seen as the first ministry partners. Just like many ministries have ministry partners today, Jesus had his ministry partners back then.

As recorded by Paul in I Corinthians, those that preach the gospel should live of the gospel. Jesus and his disciples had all of their needs met and had more than enough to give to the poor through their ministry partners during his three and a half year ministry. They always had more than enough and never lacked anything.

Let's take a look when a large crowd had gathered and had been with Jesus for several days. They are all hungry and the disciples tell Jesus he should simply send them away for them to find their own food. Jesus disagrees...

> *"Send them away, that they may go into the country round about, and into the villages, and buy themselves bread: for they have nothing to eat. He answered and said unto them, Give ye them to eat. And they say unto him, <u>Shall we go and buy</u> two hundred pennyworth of bread, and give them to eat?"*
> Mark 6:36-37

Jesus tells them to feed the people. The disciples ask him, "Are you sure, do you really want us to go buy that much bread for all these people?" Notice the disciples never said, "We can't afford that much bread." They didn't say anything like that. They said, "Shall we go and buy…Are you sure you want us to go buy that much bread?"

I'm sure the disciples were thinking, "Where in the world do you think we're going to get that much bread?" They can't just run down to the local Wal-Mart Supercenter to get it. No store in town is going have anywhere near that much available for them to buy. They're shocked and have no idea where in the world they're supposed to get it even though they have the money for it.

In this case, when there is no way possible to find a place to buy that much bread, Jesus does the miraculous. The food is multiplied and everyone eats until they're completely full. When the natural isn't enough (nowhere to buy that much food), God does the supernatural to supply all the needs of the people.

> *"And they did eat, and were all filled: and there was taken up of fragments that remained to them twelve baskets."*
> Luke 9:17

When they finished eating, there were twelve baskets of food left over. I love this. Notice that when God gives supernatural supply, He doesn't just give the people enough food to eat. He gives them too much! God is a God of Abundance. He is the not the God of lack. Nor is He the God of just enough. He is El Shaddai, the God who is more than enough. He provided more than enough food for everyone.

Jesus Was a Well Dressed Man

> *"Then the soldiers, when they had crucified Jesus, took his garments, and made four parts, to every soldier a part; and also his coat: <u>now the coat was without seam, woven from the top throughout</u>. They said therefore among themselves, Let us not rend it, but cast lots for it, whose it shall be: that the scripture might be fulfilled, which saith, They parted my raiment among them, and <u>for my vesture they did cast lots</u>. These things therefore the soldiers did."*

John 19:23-24

The Roman soldiers divided up Jesus' clothes when he was crucified. They also cast lots for his coat since it was one seamless garment. Would the Roman soldiers have taken the time to gamble over a worthless bunch of rags? No. They were only gambling over his clothes because it was a very nice and valuable garment. So all the soldiers wanted it and had to cast lots to see who the winner was going to be for it.

They weren't gambling over the rags of a beggar. They were gambling over some valuable clothing all of them wanted.

Chapter Five
Jesus Became Poor So You Could Become Rich

> *"For ye know the grace of our Lord Jesus Christ, that, though he was rich, yet for your sakes he became poor, that ye through his poverty might be rich."*
> 2 Corinthians 8:9

> *"For you are becoming progressively acquainted with and recognizing more strongly and clearly the grace of our Lord Jesus Christ (His kindness, His gracious generosity, His undeserved favor and spiritual blessing), [in] that though He was [so very] rich, yet for your sakes He became [so very] poor, in order that by His poverty you might become enriched (<u>abundantly supplied</u>)."*
> 2 Corinthians 8:9, AMP

I love the way the Amplified reads on this Bible verse. It defines being rich as "abundantly supplied." I personally define rich as, "Having more than enough to accomplish my full and complete purpose here on earth." The majority of believers will only accomplish a small portion of what God has called them to do. Very few of them go all the way with God and accomplish everything He has called them to do.

Sometimes they don't complete their purpose because they're not committed enough. Other things get their attention. Distractions come in and pull them away from God. Other times they never seek God to find out the purpose for their life. And still others know the plan and are reaching for it, but they never have the finances it takes to accomplish living and doing everything God has called for them to do.

Through the sacrifice of Jesus, God has abundantly supplied you with everything you will ever need to accomplish your purpose here on earth. You don't need to beg for it. You don't need to cry about it. And you definitely don't need to be fearful of it. Everything you will ever need in life has been abundantly supplied to you through the sacrifice of Jesus.

Jesus Substituted Himself In Your Place

What happened at the cross? Did Jesus just atone for your sins like the animals were used to atone for sin in the Old Testament? Did he simply go to the cross as a sacrifice to forgive you for your sin? No...a thousand times NO. God has definitely forgiven you for your sins through the cross, but He has done so much more than that for you.

Many believers treat the blood of Jesus as not much better than the blood of animals sacrificed in the Old Covenant. If you sinned under the Old Covenant (and everybody has sinned and come short of the glory of God), then you would sacrifice an animal to the Lord to atone for your sin. You would bring the animal to the priest (different animals were used for different types of sacrifices). The animal would be killed and its blood would be used on the altar to atone for the sin you committed.

You would receive forgiveness before God for your sin. Something always had to die to atone for sin. The wages of sin is death. Every sin brings death and separation from God. You would be sacrificing this animal in your place to die for the sin you committed.

> *"For the life of the flesh is in the blood: and I have given it to you upon the altar to make an atonement for your souls: for <u>it is the blood that maketh an atonement for the soul</u>."*
> Leviticus 17:11

The life of the flesh is the blood. Life is in the blood. The blood of this animal would be taken and used on the altar and you would be forgiven of your sin before God. God would no longer look at you as having committed the sin because the animal has taken your place in death for the sin. The sacrifices of the Old Covenant were to atone for sin. Atonement throughout the Old Testament is the word, "kaphar" and it means, "to cover." The blood of bulls and goats was used to cover our sins. Each time you sinned you would have to sacrifice another animal to the Lord in your place. God would accept your sacrifice and the sin would be covered by the blood of this animal's death.

The word atonement is only used one time in the New Testament. When it is used, it has a completely different definition than the Old Covenant had. It is the Greek word, "chaph" and it means, "pure." This is because Jesus' blood doesn't just cover us from sin. It goes much further than this.

> *"And not only so, but we also joy in God through our Lord Jesus Christ, by whom we have now received the atonement."*
> Romans 5:11

The sacrifices in the Old Covenant simply covered our sins. Jesus' blood has made us pure from sin just as if sin never existed in our lives before. In the Old Covenant, no one could enter the Holy of Holies (the very presence of God) except once per year when the High Priest entered the Holy of Holies on the Day of Atonement to make an offering for the sins of all the people.

Even after making a sacrifice for sin and having sin covered in their lives, they were still not holy before God. Sinful man could not stand in the presence of a Holy God. The individual sins could be taken care of and covered, but the sin nature in man remained. This sinful nature was inherited from Adam and is what has created the drive in us to sin.

"Wherefore, as <u>by one man sin entered into the world</u>, and death by sin; and so death passed upon all men, for that all have sinned:"
Romans 5:12

When Adam sinned in the Garden of Eden, he chose to follow Satan instead of God. The Lord said that the day he ate of the Tree of Knowledge of Good and Evil, he would die. He didn't die physically that day, but his spirit died. He was instantly separated from the nature of God and took on a sin nature. Death does not mean cease to exist. When you die in this body, you don't cease to exist. The moment you die you will either go to Heaven or Hell based on whether you've accepted Christ's sacrifice for you. You don't disappear out of existence. Physical death simply means you are separated from your body.

Adam died spiritually that day which simply means he was separated from the life of God. He could no longer be free in the presence of God. Fear immediately took over in his life. He knew he was naked and he hid himself from the presence of God. The nature of God (which is love) no longer ruled in his life. Selfishness took its place.

Every person has received this sinful nature passed down through Adam. This is why we have all sinned and come short of the glory of God. Sin is a part of our very being. Even a Pharisee of Pharisees such as Paul who did his best to follow the Law in every way could never escape from his own sin nature.

"For I know that in me (that is, in my flesh,) dwelleth no good thing: for to will is present with me; but how to perform that which is good I find not. For the good that I would I do not: but the evil which I would not, that I do. Now if I do that I would not, it is no more I that do it, but <u>sin that dwelleth in me</u>."
Romans 7:18-20

Paul records here that when he was trying to follow the Law he was not able to do so. He wanted to do good. Yet, he did not have the ability to do good. Doing good simply wasn't part of him. He didn't want to do evil things, yet he would still end up doing them. He couldn't seem to help himself. The sin nature that was a part of him made him do those things. Everybody who hasn't been born again has those same struggles going on inside them. They may want to quit taking drugs, but they just can't. The drugs are too strong for them. If they go through rehabilitation, they may get free for a while, but the drugs will eventually suck them right back in again.

The majority of prisoners who get paroled will end up right back in jail in just a few years. They may have spent time in jail and they will tell you they don't ever want to go back there again. But they just can't help themselves, the sinful nature will begin pulling on them again as soon as they're out and it isn't too long until they're back at their old ways. That old sinful nature is just too strong for them.

Sin is just like a disease. In the Old Testament, it was treated just like medicine may treat a disease. You sinned. You would sacrifice an animal so your sin could be covered. You'd sin again. You'd make another sacrifice. The process would continue year after year because the root cause of the problem had never been dealt with. It was only being covered up.

If someone has skin cancer, they can use makeup to cover it up. Then others won't see it. It will keep growing and they can keep covering it up. While you won't see the problem, it is still in them. They can cover up the problem all they want, but it still does its damage to them. Just covering it up won't deal with it. It has to be cured.

The sacrifice of Christ was the cure to do away with the disease. His blood doesn't just cover up your sin. His sacrifice has gone down to the root of sin in you. He has destroyed and put to death the sin nature on the inside of you. You are no longer a slave to sin and forced to serve it by your inner nature. You have been made free from it by the blood of Jesus. When you give your heart to God and accept Jesus as your Savior, you receive a brand new nature on the inside of you.

The whole book of Hebrews is about this subject. Many people find Hebrews to be a difficult book to understand, but its basis is in the difference between Old Covenant sacrifices and the New Covenant sacrifice Jesus made with his own blood. It's about how much better His sacrifice is. Old Covenant sacrifices simply covered up our sins and had to be made continually every year because they were so limited in value. The blood of Jesus has been offered one time and has completely dealt with sin once and for all.

> *"For since the Law has merely a rude outline (foreshadowing) of the good things to come--instead of fully expressing those things--it can never by offering the same sacrifices continually year after year make perfect those who approach [its altars]. For if it were otherwise, would [these sacrifices] not have stopped being offered? Since the worshipers had once for all been cleansed, they would no longer have any guilt or consciousness of sin. But [as it is] these sacrifices annually bring a fresh remembrance of sins [to be atoned for], Because the <u>blood of bulls and goats is powerless to take sins away</u>."*
> Hebrews 10:1-4, AMP

> *"Furthermore, every [human] priest stands [at his altar of service] ministering daily, offering the same sacrifices over and over again, which <u>never are able to strip</u> [from every side of us] <u>the sins</u> [that envelop us] and take them away--Whereas this one [Christ], after He had offered a single sacrifice for our sins [that shall avail] for all time, sat down at the right hand of God, Then to wait until His enemies should be made a stool beneath His feet. [Ps 110:1.] For by a single offering <u>He has forever completely cleansed and perfected</u> those who are consecrated and made holy."*

Hebrews 10:11-14, AMP

The sacrifices of the Law had to be made continually year after year because they were not dealing with the root problem of sin. They were simply covering up sin. The blood of bulls and goats was powerless to take away sin. All they could do is cover up sin. The sin nature in man remained so he stayed a sinful creature in bondage to his own desires.

Jesus made one sacrifice for sin forever. Then he sat down at the right hand of God waiting until all his enemies were made his footstool. With one sacrifice, he has forever completely cleansed and perfected our inner man. We have become new creatures on the inside and sin no longer has dominion over us. We are FREE!

> *"For the love of Christ constraineth us; because we thus judge, that if <u>one died for all, then were all dead</u>: And that he died for all, that they which live should not henceforth live unto themselves, but unto him which died for them, and rose again. Wherefore henceforth know we no man after the flesh: yea, though we have known Christ after the flesh, yet now henceforth know we him no more. Therefore if any man be in Christ, <u>he is a new creature</u>: old things are passed away; behold, all things are become new. And all things are of God, who hath reconciled us to himself by Jesus Christ, and hath given to us the ministry of reconciliation; To wit, that God was in Christ, reconciling the world unto himself, not imputing their trespasses unto them; and hath committed unto us the word of reconciliation. Now then we are ambassadors for Christ, as though God did beseech you by us: we pray you in Christ's stead, be ye reconciled to God. For <u>he hath made him to be sin for us</u>, who knew no sin; that <u>we might be made the righteousness of God in him</u>."*
> 2 Corinthians 5:14-21

Up until now you have been learning what Jesus did and how it was different from Old Testament sacrifices. This passage teaches how Jesus has dealt with our sin natures and how He has set us free. The term for this is substitution and identification. Jesus took our place and became our substitute so we could receive His nature inside of us.

Jesus went to the cross and He died in your place for your sin. The Old Testament sacrifices were a shadow of this. When you sinned in the Old Covenant, an animal would be killed in your place for God to cover your sin. Jesus has done the same thing, but he took it much further. Instead of just dying for individual sins you have committed, he died for your entire sin nature.

Verse twenty-one reveals that God has made Jesus to be sin for us. He didn't just carry specific sins you've committed. He became sin. If He had only been sacrificed for specific sins, then he would have to be sacrificed again and again throughout eternity just like Old Testament sacrifices. Instead, God went right to the heart of the problem and laid sin itself on Jesus.

Jesus had never committed sin. He lived perfect before both God and man. He was the only one to fulfill and never break a single commandment of the Law during his entire life. Because of the virgin birth, he had never been born with a sin nature like the rest of humanity. Life is in the blood and Jesus was born of a virgin so he never received sin tainted human blood.

Mankind was separated from God by sin. Man could not enter God's presence to fellowship with him. Jesus lived his whole life in the presence of God in total, complete fellowship with the ruler of the universe. He lived in the same fellowship with God Adam had before he gave it up.

He was the perfect sacrifice. The perfect spotless Lamb of God took our place and became sin. He took our separation from God. While he was hanging on the cross, he cried out, "Father why have you forsaken me." For the only time in eternity, Jesus and the Father were separated on the cross. The earth became pitch black for three hours while he hung there completely separated from the presence of God. All of God's judgment on sin was poured out on Jesus in your place.

God was satisfied. The penalty of sin was completed in Jesus for you. II Corinthians 5:14 says that if one died for all, then all were dead. God looks at you and sees you as having died with him. That old nature of sin which was in you was put to death on the cross. It was fully dealt with and done away with. Old things have passed away.

You may have been a drug addict. You may have been a thief. You may have been a liar. You may have been a fornicator. You may have been a murderer. You may have been a glutton. You may have used to be those things and more, but you died. Your old sinful nature died with Jesus on the cross.

Sin used to drive you. That selfish nature you inherited from Adam forced you to do those things. But when you accepted Jesus as your Lord and Savior, you died on the cross with him. You have been "born again" into a brand new life. You have become a new creature altogether. All things have been made new in you by God.

God removed the selfish nature of Adam from you and has put His own love nature into you. You can no longer do the things you used to. If you try to do the sins from your "old man," you will immediately feel conviction taking place in your heart. Those things are simply not a part of you anymore. Look at this part of II Corinthians 5 again in the Amplified version...

> "But all things are from God, Who through Jesus Christ reconciled us to Himself [received us into favor, <u>brought us into harmony with Himself</u>] and gave to us the ministry of reconciliation [that by word and deed we might aim to bring others into harmony with Him]. It was God [personally present] in Christ, reconciling and restoring the world to favor with Himself, <u>not counting up and holding against [men] their trespasses</u> [but cancelling them], and committing to us the message of reconciliation (of the restoration to favor). So we are Christ's ambassadors, God making His appeal as it were

through us. We [as Christ's personal representatives] beg you for His sake to lay hold of the divine favor [now offered you] and be <u>reconciled to God</u>."
2 Corinthians 5:18-20, AMP

God reconciled us to Himself through Jesus Christ. He brought us into harmony and agreement with Himself. He has made peace with you. He isn't angry at you. All of His righteous anger on sin was taken out on Jesus at the cross. He has brought you into peace with Himself. God looks at you and He sees His own Son in you (having never sinned). You are made in His image and have received His nature. You are His child.

Righteousness is a difficult word to understand sometimes as you go through the New Testament. It simply means you are in right relationship with God. Jesus was righteous. Through his sacrifice, that righteousness has been given to you. You are now righteous. You are in right relationship with God just as if sin never existed.

Now here is where some people get upset. You are no less righteous than Jesus was. Jesus is no more righteous than you are. Why? Because you're not living in your own righteousness, you have been given His. Your righteousness would have been as filthy rags. You could never stand in the presence of God on your own merits, but you have been given Jesus' own standing with God.

We have been called as ambassadors for God to share this message with the world. It is the Gospel (Good News). God is no longer counting or holding their sins against them. God is not mad at them. They have been forgiven. They have been restored to God's favor and love already. All they have to do is accept Jesus Christ's free gift and make peace with God themselves.

We can walk right up into the presence of God now. In the Old Covenant, no one but the High Priest could enter the Holy of Holies (the very presence of God). And He could only enter once per year. We have been made righteous and can come boldly to the throne of grace (Heb 4:16). We can walk right up to the throne of God through prayer. We are no longer separated from Him by our sin nature.

When Jesus died on the cross, the veil of the temple was ripped from the top to the bottom. God was no longer going to dwell in a temple made with hands. A veil would no longer separate us from His presence. Now He has taken up residence inside of everyone who has accepted Him. We have been made the temple of God ourselves and He lives in us (II Cor 6:16).

The blood of Jesus has done much more for you than simply forgiving you of sin. It has removed the old sinful nature from you as your old man died with Him. It has replaced that nature with a brand new nature created for you by God. Your old standing of wretchedness has been removed and you have been given Jesus' own righteousness (right standing with God). Because you are a new creature, God has made you His own temple and has moved into you. You are now free from sin and it no longer has any dominion over you.

But Brother Dean, I'm Not Free

Anytime you teach people the Word, you'll have someone say, "Brother Dean, I'm born again, but I still have a problem with sin. I don't seem to be free from it at all." Yes, I know you have a problem with sin you little flesh creature. A born again Christian can still sin. It's just not a part of their nature anymore.

The problem with you is your mind hasn't been renewed yet. You have been given a new nature and you are free from sin, but you're still walking around with an unrenewed mind bound by your past. It is full of hurts, confusion, and mistakes. You have to take the Word of God and use it to clean your mind of every past idea you've had about yourself.

"*And be not conformed to this world: but be ye transformed by the renewing of your mind, that ye may*

prove what is that good, and acceptable, and perfect, will of God."
Romans 12:2

"(For the weapons of our warfare are not carnal, but mighty through God to the <u>pulling down of strong holds</u>;) Casting down imaginations, and every high thing that exalteth itself against the knowledge of God, and <u>bringing into captivity every thought</u> to the obedience of Christ;"
2 Corinthians 10:4-5

Your mind needs to be renewed. It needs to be renovated just like you would take an old house and fix it up. Your spirit inside of you has been changed, but you are still walking around with the same old mind. It's your job to take over this project and renovate your mind (and some of us have some big projects ahead of us). When you start renewing your mind, you will be transformed into someone who walks in the good, acceptable, and perfect will of God.

The renovation project on your mind requires you to pull down all the strongholds of wrong thinking. You have to cast down imaginations and everything that works against the knowledge of God. Every thought must be brought into captivity to the Word of God. The wrong ideas you have about God must be brought down. You may have thought God was mad at you. You may have thought He was the one making people poor. You may have thought He put problems and sickness in your life to teach you something. All of those wrong ideas must be destroyed through the Word of God.

The wrong ideas about yourself have to be brought down. You may still call yourself a worthless worm. You may see yourself as just a sinner saved by grace. You may see yourself as a failure. You may see yourself as stupid. You may be thinking all these things about yourself right now, but they have to be brought down. You have to begin to see yourself the way God sees you. He sees you as a victorious champion in life walking in His full power and wisdom just like Jesus did.

Later on this in this book you'll learn exactly how you can use the Word of God to clean and renew your mind. You'll learn how to change your stinking thinking into something God can use. You'll learn more about how you can experience everything God has for you by putting yourself in position to receive from Him.

Just Like Jesus Became Sin, He Became Poor In Your Place

"For ye know the grace of our Lord Jesus Christ, that, though he was rich, yet for your sakes he became poor, that ye through his poverty might be rich."
2 Corinthians 8:9

Though Jesus was rich (abundantly supplied), he became poor for your sake. Poor in this verse is the Greek word, "ptocheuo" which means, "to be as poor as a beggar, to be destitute." Jesus never spent one day in poverty in heaven or on the earth. He never had to go a single day without every financial blessing. All He had to do was pray to the Father, and He would have received anything he requested.

Then he began his substitutionary work. He gave up all the wealth available to Him. He gave up the Father's presence. He gave up His righteous standing with God. No man could take his life. He laid it down. He gave up all of His heavenly righteous standing with God for you. He gave up His riches for you.

He took your place in sin when he died on the cross. He took your poverty as He went to the cross. He was rich, yet He became poor. He became as poor as a beggar. While He was on the cross, they were even gambling for the clothing He wore. Everything was stripped from Him completely.

No matter how poor you may be today, God laid your poverty on Jesus. He then turned around and gave you Jesus' standing. He gave you His riches and the full backing of heaven in your life. You never have to experience lack in your life again. You have abundant provision available to you from God.

He has given you the standing of "rich" by grace just like He gave you the standing of righteousness by grace. It is by unmeritable, unearnable favor. He gave you this standing as a free gift. You did nothing to earn it. You will never in your life do anything to earn it. The moment you are born again you have all of heaven backing you. In God's eyes, you are abundantly supplied for everything you will ever need on this earth.

Heirs of God and Joint-Heirs With Jesus Christ

"For as many as are led by the Spirit of God, they are the sons of God. For ye have not received the spirit of bondage again to fear; but ye have received the Spirit of adoption, whereby we cry, Abba, Father. The Spirit itself beareth witness with our spirit, that we are the children of God: And if children, then heirs; heirs of God, and joint-heirs with Christ; if so be that we suffer with him, that we may be also glorified together."
Romans 8:14-17

"For whom he did foreknow, he also did predestinate to be conformed to the image of his Son, that he might be the firstborn among many brethren."
Romans 8:29

You are a child of God. You are a son/daughter of God. You're not the Son of God, but you are a son of God. You have been given that standing in the family. God is your Father and Jesus is your firstborn older brother. Talk about a family tree!

God has taken you, someone who used to be a sinner, and has adopted you into His own family. You have been born again into this new family and we are all brothers and sisters in Christ. You're not black sheep of the family either. You are a full son of God. He treats you and loves you the exact same way He did Jesus.

So say it right now with your mouth. Say, "God loves me just as much as He loves Jesus." Say it again. Take time saying that throughout the day. God loves you...and it's not some wimpy, second class love either. When He looks at you, He sees the righteousness bestowed on you by Jesus. He sees you as a full son that has never sinned before.

Sometimes preachers try to take the word "adoption" from the Romans passage above to make us seem to be like second class family members. Adoption is a Greek word that is only used in the Bible during Paul's writings. It is "huiothesia" and it is the combination of two Greek words. The first one means, "a son." The second one means, "to place." So Paul's use of adoption simply means that God took you and moved you from being a sinner into being a son. You were originally somewhere else, and then God placed you as a son.

One of the Holy Spirit's primary jobs in our lives is to reveal what Jesus has done for us and in us. Here He is called the "Spirit of Adoption" because He is helping us realize our family relationship. He is bringing us to the knowledge that God is not just God to us. He is our beloved and dear Father. Your mind can never conceive the reality of this by itself. It is only by revelation of the Holy Spirit that it can sink down into your consciousness. God is your Father. You are His child.

Since you are His child, then you are also His heir. You're an heir of God and a joint-heir with Jesus Christ. Everything the Father has is yours. He repeats Himself over and over again throughout the New Testament that whatever you ask Him for, He will give it to you.

> *"And in that day ye shall ask me nothing. Verily, verily, I say unto you, <u>Whatsoever ye shall ask the Father in my name, he will give it you</u>. Hitherto have ye asked nothing in my name: ask, and ye shall receive, <u>that your joy may be full</u>. These things have I spoken unto you in proverbs: but the time cometh, when I shall no more speak unto you*

in proverbs, but I shall shew you plainly of the Father. At that day ye shall ask in my name: and I say not unto you, that I will pray the Father for you: For <u>the Father himself loveth you</u>, because ye have loved me, and have believed that I came out from God."
John 16:23-27

    The Father will give you whatever you ask Him for in the name of Jesus. That is exciting! Whatever you ask for, you will receive from Him. He is a good Daddy. He wants to give good gifts to his children. Look why He will give you what you ask for, "that your joy may be full." He wants to see you full of joy, because He loves you.

    Pretend you're a parent getting ready for Christmas. Your child asked you for a very specific present they desperately wanted and you worked hard to do it (all that running around shopping at the stores), but you got them the exact one they wanted. You wait until Christmas and you watch the expression of excitement and joy as they open up their present. You get excited just to see the joy on their face, don't you?

    Last Christmas I went shopping with my mother-in-law to buy my wife all kinds of presents. I could insert a mother-in-law joke here, but I actually get along with mine. I bought my wife over a dozen different presents. There were large presents, small presents, and all types of presents. We wrapped them up and waited for Christmas. I simply couldn't stand it anymore. I couldn't wait all the way to Christmas. I started giving her a present just about everyday for two weeks before Christmas. I loved to see her joy when she opened her presents. So everyday I wanted to give her something else. It made me happy to see her "joy full."

    That is how God is to us. He wants to give you what you ask Him for because you are his beloved child. He wants to see that expression of joy on your face when you get it. He wants to hear you say, "Thank you Daddy." He wants to give to you. He is Love and the very nature of Love is to be a giver. God is the biggest giver there is. So make your Father happy and start receiving from Him.

For too long we've had a totally wrong attitude about our Father. We've seen Him as an angry God just waiting for us to do something wrong so He can bust our heads. We've been afraid of our Father. We haven't trusted our Father to keep his word. Our Father tells us He wants to give us something, and we run around not quite sure if He'll give it to us.

Let's take another visual image. Pretend you're a child and you have a loving father who has never lied to you or any of your brothers or sisters. He is a man of integrity and is very wealthy. He tells you he is going to take you to Disneyworld next week. So you go to school all excited and tell all your friends you're going to Disneyworld.

Have you seen Disneyworld? Nope. Do you have the tickets in your hand? Nope. Do you have any proof you're going to Disneyworld? Nope. You tell everyone you're going to Disneyworld because you know and trust your father. You simply believe because you know the character of your father.

Johnny, your best friend, tells you not to get your hopes up too high. He tells you how his father said they were going to Disneyworld last year and then he had to go on a business trip instead. Susan tells you a similar story about how her father was supposed to take her to Sea World, but the car broke down and had to be repaired instead. All day long different kids at school tell you not to get your hopes up because of how their fathers have failed to give them what they promised.

None of that stops you or even moves you off your confession that you're going to Disneyworld. You believe you're going because your father said you're going...and he has never lied to you. Now, if you had a dad who did lie (like many have had), then you wouldn't be as sure of yourself...especially when the "persecution" came. You would begin to doubt your father, because your father's track record wasn't so sure. You may be afraid you weren't going to Disneyworld after all.

It all matters who your dad is, what his character is, and just how well you know him. A lot of us simply haven't known our heavenly Father that well. It is impossible for Him to lie. It is impossible for Him to fail. It is impossible for Him not to have the resources to accomplish His promise. Whatever He has promised, He will do. He has promised to give you whatever you ask for in Jesus name. He has made you an heir to His kingdom. He is eagerly waiting for you to find this out so He can see the pleasure and joy on your face when He gives you what you're asking for.

Say this, "God is my Father and I'm an heir to everything He has. God loves giving me good gifts so my joy can be full. Nothing is too big for Him."

Just How Rich Is Your Daddy?

"For the earth is the Lord's, and the fulness thereof."
1 Corinthians 10:26

"Who hath prevented me, that I should repay him? whatsoever is under the whole heaven is mine."
Job 41:11

"For every beast of the forest is mine, and the cattle upon a thousand hills."
Psalms 50:10

You've been born again into a new family. You should take some time to find out all the assets your family has available. The verses above give a pretty good starting point for you. The whole earth and everything that is in it is the Lord's. Everything under the whole heaven is owned by the family. Every beast in the forest and all the cattle in the world are His. You're not serving a broke, barely making it God. He is not wasteful, but He is definitely not a miser either. When some overly religious people get to heaven, they'll probably throw fits at God's decorating habits. Heaven has streets of gold and a gate that is made out of one huge pearl.

Because of God's blessing and His gift of wisdom to Solomon, everything they had was made of gold. All the drinking vessels were even of gold. Silver wasn't counted as worth anything because there was so much gold in the kingdom. Does it sound like God has a problem with wealth? No...definitely not. God created the diamonds. He created the gold. He created all the precious stones. He created a world with riches and wealth in it that we have only begun to tap into so far.

God has never had a problem with wealth. It is one of the blessings He longs to provide His children with. He wants you to have wealth. He just doesn't want wealth to have you. Seek His kingdom first, and all these things will be added unto you.

The Prodigal Son's Brother

Let's go to a common parable of Jesus. It is in Luke 15 and you can read it in its entirety there. It's the Parable of the Prodigal Son. The prodigal son asked his father to give him the portion of goods that belonged to him. He wanted to enjoy it while he was still young.

He partied and spent it all until there was nothing left. He was away from home and flat broke. He got himself a job feeding pigs and ended up stealing some of their food just to survive. Finally he came to his senses and realized his father had many servants he took good care of. They never went hungry and were well provided for. So he got up and went home to ask his father to make him a hired servant.

When his father saw him coming down the road, he was ecstatic with joy and ran out to hug him. The father brought his best robe, family ring, and shoes to clothe his lost son. They killed a calf and had a wonderful time because his son that was lost had come back.

The prodigal son's brother was angry and wouldn't have anything to do with the excitement. He was mad that the whole time he had been living with the father; the father never killed a calf and had a party for him. He felt like his father loved the prodigal son more even though he was the one who had been faithful to his father. The elder didn't feel he had ever received this good of treatment after all of his obedience. That harlot loving, money wasting prodigal son got something he never received. Look at the father's response to him…

> *"And he said unto him, Son, thou art ever with me, and <u>all that I have is thine.</u>"*
> Luke 15:31

Everything the father had was his. He could have killed a calf and had a party with his friends anytime he wanted. He could have worn one of the robes and put a ring on his finger anytime. It was all his. Everything the father had was his. He just never knew his father well enough to realize it.

The Prodigal Son's brother never spent enough time with his father to realize everything the father had was his.

In this story, the Father is our Father God. The prodigal son is anyone out of relationship with Him. The Father rejoices and has a party anytime a new person comes to Christ for the first time or comes back to him from being lost. Jesus said He was the good shepherd and would leave the sheep to go after the one that was lost. It's a joy filled time to God when anyone gives their heart to Him.

This brother though is symbolic of the believer who gets mad about God showering his blessings on a new convert. He sees the joy on their face and tells them it just won't last. He sees them receive blessings from heaven such as a physical healing or a financial blessing, and he gets mad about it. He goes to God and tells Him it's not fair. He has worked in the church for 20 years and has never received a healing in his body. He has been faithful with giving finances into God's work and he has never seen any financial miracles.

This upset believer sits down on the pew and cries out to God, "Why do you love this brand new believer who used to be a prostitute more than me when I've spent the last 20 years of my life serving you?" If Jesus was still on the earth, he would give this believer the same answer the father gave his son, "All I have is yours..."

They may have worked in the church, but they obviously haven't spent enough time in prayer and in the Word getting to know their Father. Otherwise they would have learned none of God's blessing come through works. They come by grace through faith.

> *"For by grace are ye saved through faith; and that not of yourselves: it is the <u>gift of God</u>: <u>Not of works</u>, lest any man should boast."*
> Ephesians 2:8-9

You are saved by grace through your faith. Jesus is the one who did the work for your salvation. You simply believe and act on the promise of God. You believe in your heart and you confess with your mouth the Lordship of Jesus to be saved. It is not based on your works. You could have been the worst murderer on the planet or an upstanding citizen. It doesn't matter. Jesus died for you and everything we receive from God is based on His sacrifice, not your works.

Every blessing you receive from God comes in the exact same way. It comes by grace through faith. You can't earn it and you will never deserve it. Your Father wants to give to you and bless you simply because you're His child. The more time you spend getting to know Him, the more you will realize that.

All of the works you do are simply a response of gratitude to the free gifts He has given you. You are grateful for everything He has provided, and you give your life to serve such a wonderful God. Those works you do for Him are never the basis for anything you receive from Him though.

The only basis for His blessings is the cross of Jesus…nothing else.

Everything the Father has is yours.

Chapter Six
The Giving Heart of a Son

> *"For ye know the <u>grace</u> of our Lord Jesus Christ, that, though he was rich, yet for your sakes he became poor, that ye through his poverty might be rich."*
> 2 Corinthians 8:9

God has made you rich (abundantly supplied). He has given you more than enough to accomplish your full and complete purpose here on earth. It's all available to you right now because of the sacrifice Jesus made for you at the cross. He became poor so you would be made rich. You never have to suffer lack in your life again. You can be abundantly supplied financially.

The keyword to this verse above is grace. Why are you made rich? It is simply because of His grace. You don't merit it and you could never earn it on your own. It is simply a grace gift from your Father accomplished through Jesus for you. It's yours right this minute. All you have to do is reach out by faith and receive it.

> *"O foolish Galatians, who hath bewitched you, that ye should not obey the truth, before whose eyes Jesus Christ hath been evidently set forth, crucified among you? This only would I learn of you<u>, Received ye the Spirit by the works of the law, or by the hearing of faith</u>? Are ye so foolish? having begun in the Spirit, are ye now made perfect by the flesh? Have ye suffered so many things in vain? if it be yet in vain. He therefore that ministereth to you the Spirit, and worketh miracles among you, doeth he it by the works of the law, or by the hearing of faith? Even as Abraham <u>believed</u> God, and it was accounted to him for righteousness."*
> Galatians 3:1-6

We have to be very careful we never turn any of Gods free gifts into something we can earn on our own merits. You don't earn your salvation. It is a free gift. Jesus went to the cross and suffered in your place for your sins. You simply receive this gift from Him and then walk in it.

You will begin to walk in His love and His commandments simply as an outflow of faith in what He has done for you. Your life will start changing because of the change that has taken place in your heart already. You will be filled with gratitude and will thank Him by living and giving your life for Him.

At no time does the change in your life mean you've now earned salvation or any of the other gifts of God. For example, many churches still believe and preach you need to get your life cleaned up before the Holy Spirit will come in you. That is a lie. He is willing to move in whenever you will let Him. Simply ask Him to come into you and then He will help you get the rest of your life cleaned up. That's His job.

You don't earn any of God's grace. He gives it to you and then the faith and gratitude in your heart cause you to walk out what you have received from Him. You may be a mess when you first receive Him. He accepts you just as you are, with all your warts and everything. No matter what kind of evil things you have done, you can still decide to receive Him into your heart today. He is standing beside you waiting for the chance to enter your life.

After you accept Him, then He moves into your heart and begins working on you. You begin feeling His love in you. That hard heart starts changing in you. You begin to feel love for others and He begins tearing down the bondages sin has created in your life. You are changed instantly, but the rest of this process takes time as He works on you. For some of us, He has a major job on His hands.

People begin seeing the changes in you. All of this happens AFTER you receive His free gift in your life. You don't clean yourself up. He cleans you up and frees you from sin. It is simply you receiving what He has done for you. So if you have never given your heart to Him, you can do it right now where you are. I don't care what you've done in your past or even what you've done today. God loves you and the blood of Jesus is more than enough to free you from any bondage in your life. Receive Him into your heart now.

When people believe they must get cleaned up before they come to Him, they'll never make it. They can't. They simply don't have the ability to be good enough to earn their salvation. There isn't a heavenly bank account that they can do this many good deeds and earn their salvation. They can't earn it. It is a gift. Many people have died in religion believing they are simply doing enough good works to make it to heaven. It is impossible. The only way to heaven is through Jesus Christ. He is the door and every other method is a liar and a thief.

Our financial blessing from God is received the same way...by grace. A mistake many Christians fall into is believing they have to do something before they earn God's favor on their finances. Most often they believe they need to give a certain amount of money first before God will bless their finances. They believe it is their giving that causes God to want to prosper them. This is just as wrong as believing it is your good works that cause you to go to heaven.

It is a mockery of the grace of God. He became poor so you might be made rich. He is the one who did the work, not you. He is the one who earned God's favor on your finances, not you. Your giving is the result of the natural change in your mindset and the gratitude in your heart for His free gift. This is exactly like your salvation. He gives you the free gift, and because of the faith and gratitude in your heart, it causes you to do the works.

Faith Without Corresponding Action is Dead

> *"What doth it profit, my brethren, though a man say he hath faith, and have not works? can faith save him? If a brother or sister be naked, and destitute of daily food, And one of you say unto them, Depart in peace, be ye*

warmed and filled; notwithstanding ye give them not those things which are needful to the body; what doth it profit? Even so <u>faith, if it hath not works, is dead,</u> being alone. Yea, a man may say, Thou hast faith, and I have works: shew me thy faith without thy works, and I will shew thee my faith by my works. Thou believest that there is one God; thou doest well: the devils also believe, and tremble. But wilt thou know, O vain man, that faith without works is dead? Was not Abraham our father justified by works, when he had offered Isaac his son upon the altar? <u>Seest thou how faith wrought with his works, and by works was faith made perfect?</u> And the scripture was fulfilled which saith, Abraham believed God, and it was imputed unto him for righteousness: and he was called the Friend of God. Ye see then how that by works a man is justified, and not by faith only. Likewise also was not Rahab the harlot justified by works, when she had received the messengers, and had sent them out another way? For as the body without the spirit is dead, <u>so faith without works is dead also."</u>
James 2:14-26

    It almost appears on the surface that this chapter of James disagrees with what Paul said in Galatians chapter three. He doesn't. He is just adding to it. The whole point of this passage is that faith causes the works in us. Many believers were running around claiming to believe in Jesus, yet there was no change in their lives at all. James is telling us here that if we truly believe in our hearts, you will see the fruit in us. Faith that does not produce fruit (works) is not real faith at all. It is a fake.
    If you truly believe Jesus loved you so much as to take your place in judgment so you can be free, then that faith will cause you to change your actions. If there is no change in your actions whatsoever, then you really don't believe at all. You're just lying to yourself and others.
    Let's say that I tell you I put a stick of dynamite under your chair. I also tell you that I lit it around 10 seconds ago and

it should go off in about 5 seconds or so. You tell me you believe me, but you don't do anything about it. You just sit there. Did you really believe me?

If you believed I stuck lit dynamite under your chair, you would have corresponding actions. You would get your butt up and move as fast as you could. Your sitting there proves you don't believe me. Real faith always causes action. If you really believe in the sacrifice of Jesus, we will see corresponding actions begin in your life.

Once you receive the revelation that Jesus became poor so you could be rich, we will see corresponding action. You will be so thankful for this that you'll become a giver. Your giving never earns God's grace in your life. It can't earn His grace. It is just the natural result of believing His Word and being grateful to Him for it.

You won't be giving to try and get something. You'll know that everything the Father has is yours just like the prodigal son's brother learned from his father. You already have something. You have abundance. This knowledge and revelation from God causes you to become a giver.

If you're not currently a giver, then you simply don't believe Jesus became poor so you might be made rich. You may claim to believe it, but you don't have a real heart revelation of it yet. It has not become a part of your thinking process. Your problem is you believe you've got to hold on for dear life to that dollar you have...or you may lose it at any moment. Well, be it done unto to you according to your faith as Jesus would say. If you greatly fear losing that dollar, then someday you will. If you believe in God's abundance and provision for you, your hand will open up and you'll become a giver by faith.

The majority of the church doesn't give at all except for plunking a few dollars in the offering plate once in a while. Churches around the world often close their doors because they simply don't receive enough to stay afloat. Their people are not free in their giving. They're in bondage to money. They're so afraid they won't be able to get what they want that they can't think of the needs others have.

You're in bondage when you don't feel free to give. You may think you're going to lose your money. You may feel you won't be able to pay your bills next month if you obey God. You may think you need to hoard every penny to impress the neighbors or your father (this is insecurity and fear of what others think).

Then there are some people who believe they made themselves rich. They don't believe in the grace of God. They believe their own ability made them rich. They don't want to open up their hands to give either, because they believe they're the ones who earned it. They believe they have a right to everything they earned...and forget everyone else. That kind of thinking is what you'll find with Satan's people. They simply don't realize God gave them the ability, the natural born gifts, and the health to prosper.

> *"That ye may be the children of your Father which is in heaven: for he maketh his sun to rise on the evil and on the good, and sendeth rain on the just and on the unjust."*
> Matthew 5:45

The basis of society at the time was agriculture. They needed sun and rain to profit and survive. God has given both the sun and the rain for both the good and the ungodly. So even non-Christians are not self-made people. They have still only profited because of the grace and goodness of God. Whatever ability, intelligence, or strength you were born with came from Him. He deserves to be praised for whatever good you have in your life!

Right and Wrong Giving

Did you know that it's possible to be a giver, and God not be pleased by your giving at all? You could take everything you have, sell it, give it all away to the poor, and God won't be pleased with your actions at all. You could do it all with the wrong motives in your heart, and God could not bless it.

> *"And though <u>I bestow all my goods to feed the poor</u>, and though I give my body to be burned, and have not charity, <u>it profiteth me nothing</u>."*
> 1 Corinthians 13:3

> *"Even if I dole out all that I have [to the poor in providing] food, and if I surrender my body to be burned or in order that I may glory, but have not love (God's love in me), I gain nothing."*
> 1 Corinthians 13:3, AMP

If you're giving out of any other motives besides the love of God, then you're giving out of the wrong motives. If your giving is motivated by what people think of you or by greed, then God simply is not in it. If you're giving in the weekly offering so that the pastor doesn't think there is something wrong with you or so your neighbor can see you drop something in the plate, then your heart is wrong.

> *"Take heed that ye do not your alms before men, <u>to be seen of them</u>: otherwise ye have no reward of your Father which is in heaven."*
> Matthew 6:1

I used to give so others could see me all the time. I'd see everyone else giving in an offering (or so I thought) and I'd pull out a few dollars to do my duty also. I didn't want anyone to think I was greedy or that I wasn't a giver. So I'd give my little token offering. Then I felt my conscience convict me one day as I thought, "Why am I giving in this offering?" I knew it was simply to be seen of the people there. I didn't want to look like the greedy guy not giving.

It was hard not to put something in the plate every time. I was helping a traveling minister and would often sit on the platform with him, and when the offering bucket would come around, I'd be thinking that everybody in the audience is looking at me not giving anything. All the other ministers are giving something, but they'll see me and think I don't ever give anything. Oh the shame, what will they all think of me? I was giving, but it was often lump sums and wasn't always given in offerings. You would think this was just a little thing, but I had a lot of difficulty just getting over this simple hurdle.

You cannot be giving to be seen of men. An even bigger hurdle for me to get over was not giving out of greed. Greed based giving is one of the biggest roadblocks holding back Christians who believe in prosperity. One of the most quoted scriptures at offering time in many of the churches I've attended is Luke 6:38.

> *"Give, and it shall be given unto you; good measure, pressed down, and shaken together, and running over, shall men give into your bosom. For with the same measure that ye mete withal it shall be measured to you again."*
> Luke 6:38

Preachers get excited about this verse. I've probably heard more messages preached on it than anything else...especially at offering time. Sometimes it has been taken even further and people start talking about some heavenly bank account. I've heard it taught that every time we give, God saves it all up in some heavenly bank account until the day he just pours it all back to us with interest.

God isn't a heavenly slot machine that you put money in, and wait for a multiplied return to come flying out. I call this type of giving "casino giving." You give a certain amount and expect God to bless it and multiply it back to you. It is even preached that God will give it back 30, 60 or 100 fold. So you're told to give $5 and God will give back $500 to you.

My wife and I were put into bondage with this legalistic teaching for quite a few years. We believed God would multiply our giving back to us one hundredfold. We were "believing" for $50,000, so we gave $500...again...and again....and again.

Many times we wouldn't pay our bills so we could give another $500.

That continued right up until the day I learned to start praying for wisdom. During the whole period where we believed we would get a hundredfold return on our giving, we never got it. We never even got a thirtyfold return. I would say we never got any return whatsoever. It wasn't until I started seeking God for an answer to our problem that we learned to change our praying...and change our giving.

We never saw any financial blessings whatsoever as long as we were giving out of greed. As long as we were giving to get a specific return, we just put ourselves in deeper trouble. We had bound ourselves up by legalism. I didn't expect God to help me because of His grace or because I was His son. I was expecting Him to bless me as a banker would with multiplied interest on my gifts.

I was living in works, not by grace. It was MY giving that would cause us to be free. It wasn't the free sacrifice of Jesus that we expected to bring us deliverance. We were believing in our giving (our works) to cause our freedom. Thousands of other believers have positioned themselves into the same bondage because of some teachings.

Obedience is Better Than Sacrifice

> *"Wherefore then didst thou not obey the voice of the LORD, but didst fly upon the spoil, and didst evil in the sight of the LORD? And Saul said unto Samuel, Yea, I have obeyed the voice of the LORD, and have gone the way which the LORD sent me, and have brought Agag the king of Amalek, and have utterly destroyed the Amalekites. But the people took of the spoil, sheep and oxen, the chief of the things which should have been utterly destroyed, to sacrifice unto the LORD thy God in Gilgal. And Samuel said, Hath the LORD as great delight in burnt offerings and sacrifices, as in obeying*

the voice of the LORD? Behold, to <u>obey is better than sacrifice</u>, and to hearken than the fat of rams."
1 Samuel 15:19-22

Saul was told to go and completely destroy the Amalekites. He was to destroy all the people, animals, and spoil. Those were his instructions from God, but instead he decided to keep the best of the sheep and oxen as a sacrifice to the Lord. God rejected Saul and removed the kingdom from him for his disobedience.

He also gives us a very important lesson. He says, "to obey is better than sacrifice." Your obedience is more important than the size of the offering you give to the Lord. It's not your "sacrifice" that pleases the Lord. Jesus' sacrifice already pleased Him for you. It's your obedience He requires.

If you know you should be going to college, but you give the money you saved for college away, then you're being disobedient. If God has called you to be a minister, but you go get a job and give 50% of everything you earn away, you're in disobedience. If you promised to buy your wife a new dress, yet you give her money to the pastor, then you've become a liar.

"If ye be willing and <u>obedient</u>, ye shall eat the good of the land: But if ye refuse and <u>rebel</u>, ye shall be devoured with the sword: for the mouth of the LORD hath spoken it."
Isaiah 1:19-20

Obedience is better than sacrifice. If you obey the Lord, you will eat the good of the land. If you rebel against the Lord, you will be destroyed by a sword. That sounds pretty clear to me. God prefers your obedience above everything else. You are to have a personal relationship with Him as your Father, not to see Him as the heavenly banker paying you for your works.

Let's say that a father tells their child to sweep the floor. Well, they don't like sweeping the floor, so they wash the dishes instead. Were they obedient? Will they be rewarded for their actions? No. They were being rebellious. They didn't do what they were told. Instead they decided to do something else.

The most important aspects of giving are obedience and love. Give where God leads you to give. Don't give because of greed or because of guilt. Give out of a love and a desire to honestly help people. Always spend time praying and seeking the Lord over your giving.

Remember this as we go to the next chapter...

You don't just sow money. You sow obedience and love.

Chapter Seven
What About the Hundredfold Return?

"Hearken; Behold, there went out a sower to sow: And it came to pass, as he sowed, some fell by the way side, and the fowls of the air came and devoured it up. And some fell on stony ground, where it had not much earth; and immediately it sprang up, because it had no depth of earth: But when the sun was up, it was scorched; and because it had no root, it withered away. And some fell among thorns, and the thorns grew up, and choked it, and it yielded no fruit. And other fell on good ground, and did yield fruit that sprang up and increased; and brought forth, <u>some thirty</u>, and <u>some sixty</u>, and <u>some an hundred</u>."
Mark 4:3-8

At some time in your Christian walk, you have probably been told to believe God for a hundredfold return on your giving. It is said that if you give God $100, you should expect to receive back $10,000. If you gave $10,000, you'd believe God for $1,000,000. If you gave that $1,000,000 away, you'd believe for $100,000,000. At this point, the numbers start getting astronomical.

It sounds like a good message. The Word constantly tells us that whatsoever we sow, we will reap. If we sow to the flesh (rebellion against God), we will reap corruption. If we sow to the spirit (obedience to God), we will reap life. We know whatever we sow, we reap. What about the hundredfold return? Let's look at what God says about the hundredfold return in the scriptures where it is mentioned.

This is the parable of the sower. You will find it in Matthew 13, Mark 4, and Luke 8. I'm using the version in Mark, because I think it is the most self-explanatory version. In the parable of the sower, Jesus tells us that a man went forth to sow. He is planting. Some of the seed fell on the wayside. It was eaten up by the birds. Some of the seed fell on stony ground. It began to spring up, but withered away because it didn't have much depth. Other seed fell among the thorns. The thorns choked it and it did not produce. Finally some of the seed fell in the good ground. It produced a return of thirtyfold, sixtyfold, and hundredfold.

What is Jesus telling us to sow in this parable? Is it money? What is it? Well, to the get the answer to this question, let's ask Jesus to explain just what he is sowing.

"The sower soweth the word."
Mark 4:14

Jesus says the parable is about sowing the Word of God. Our hearts are His garden and He is sowing His Word into our hearts. There are four different kinds of hearts that receive the Word of God. There are wayside hearts, stony hearts, thorny hearts, and good hearts. How you receive the Word of God determines how much fruit grows in your life.

We need to spend some time really studying this parable, because Jesus also tells us that if we don't understand this parable, we'll have trouble understanding every other parable. This is one of His most basic parables and is also the foundation for many of the others things He teaches throughout the Gospels.

"And he said unto them, Know ye not this parable? and <u>how then will ye know all parables?</u> The sower soweth the word. And these are they by the way side, where the word is sown; but when they have heard, Satan cometh immediately, <u>and taketh away the word that was sown in their hearts</u>. And these are they likewise which are sown on stony ground; who, when they have heard the word,

immediately receive it with gladness; And have no root in themselves, and so endure but for a time: afterward, when affliction or persecution ariseth for the word's sake, immediately they are offended. And these are they which are sown among thorns; such as hear the word, And the cares of this world, and the deceitfulness of riches, and the lusts of other things entering in, choke the word, and it becometh unfruitful. And these are they which are sown on good ground; such as <u>hear the word</u>, and <u>receive it</u>, and <u>bring forth fruit</u>, some thirtyfold, some sixty, and some an hundred."
Mark 4:13-20

So the seed is the Word of God. It is being sowed in our hearts. It may be sown by your minister at church. It could be sown by you listening to a preacher on your tape player on the way to work. It could be sown by watching a minister on TV as they teach or preach the Word. It may be sown as you study the Word of God on your own at home. No matter where the Word is coming from, it is being sown in your heart. Then Jesus goes on to tell us what the different kinds of ground are it can be sown in. If you want the Word of God to produce fruit in your life, then you have to make sure you become the good ground Jesus is talking about.

Satan Comes Immediately to Steal the Word

The first type of ground is the wayside ground. When the Word is heard, Satan comes immediately to steal the Word. The Word of God is our primary tool against the devil's devices. It is our sword we use to defeat him. He isn't afraid of you, man's traditions, or any made up doctrines. He is terrified of the Word of God though, and it can be used to defeat him time and time again.

So his first goal in every one of our lives is to steal the Word from us. The way Satan works in the wayside heart is by immediately coming in and bringing doubt on the Word of God.

If you are being taught about how prosperity is for you, then Satan will immediately begin bringing doubt in your mind about the message.

Satan can use religious doctrines you've been taught in the past to block the Word of God. He may say to you, "That prosperity stuff isn't for you. Remember how you were taught Jesus was poor. If he was poor, you should be poor too." Or His message to your mind might be, "That prosperity stuff isn't for you today. God doesn't prosper His people anymore." No matter what you're being taught, you can pretty much expect the Devil will try to bring doubt on it in your mind.

He may even get personal with you and say something like, "Prosperity is true for some Christians. It just isn't true for you. God has called you to be poor all your life and suffer for His glory." Satan could even use the voice of your mother saying, "You're stupid. You'll never amount to anything in life." He'll tell you about others who you thought believed the Word and failed, "Remember Uncle Bob, he tried that prosperity stuff and he went broke." He is not even above reminding you about your past, "Remember how you tried that once, and it didn't work for you."

You have to get past all of that junk to believe the Word of God. Anytime you hear a message from the Word, you're going to have thoughts like that fly through your head. That is Satan sending His little doubt messages to block the Word in your life so it doesn't bring forth any fruit. No matter what message you're hearing from the Word, you will get ideas like that floating through your mind.

You have a choice. You can believe religious doctrines you've heard in the past. You can believe what Uncle Bob says. You can believe what your parents told you. Or you can believe God. Everyone else may be good people, but only God cannot lie. It is impossible for God to lie and everything He has ever said is 100% truth. Everyone else is imperfect and isn't always right. The only way past this first roadblock Satan sets up is to believe the Word of God only. Anything or anyone who disagrees with the Word is wrong.

Affliction and Persecution Come To Steal the Word

> *"And these are they likewise which are sown on stony ground; who, when they have heard the word, immediately receive it with gladness; And have no root in themselves, and so endure but for a time: afterward, when <u>affliction or persecution ariseth for the word's sake</u>, immediately they are offended."*
> Mark 4:16-17

This is for those who have gotten past the first barrier. Satan tried to steal the Word from you, but he couldn't get it out of your heart. He used every tactic he had in his arsenal of lies, but none of them worked. You believe the Word of God to be true in spite of everything else you've heard or thought in the past.

Now Satan goes to plan B. If he can't steal the Word from you immediately, his next goal is to wear you down. He goes on the offense. He begins sending tribulation and persecution your way to get you off the Word. Notice why afflictions and persecution come in the above verse? Is it coming because of you? No. It is coming for the Word's sake.

Why does affliction come in your life? Satan uses it to steal the Word out of your heart so it never produces fruit. He will even try to lie to you and convince you the affliction you're experiencing is coming from God. If he can get you to believe that lie, he has you right where he wants you. He can send whatever he wants down the path and you'll accept it as God's will for you.

Satan has already used this tactic to deceive a majority in the body of Christ. It is a very common belief that people believe trials and tribulations come into our lives to purify us or to teach us something. That's how the liar works. If he convinces you that his work is really God working in your life, then you go into a state of non-resistance to him. You'll allow him to work in your life to his heart's content. He will systematically begin stealing the Word of God out of you through the situations of life.

You're a smart person. If Satan appeared to you in horns, a red cloak, and a pitchfork, you would immediately spot him. You'd tell him he was the devil and that he wasn't going to steal the Word of God from you. So he sneaks up on you and disguises himself as God. He tells you that he is God trying to teach you something in your life. Just sit down, shut up, and learn what he has to teach you. You then sit there and let him steal every piece of the Word of God that you knew allowing him to replace each one with a tradition of man.

> *"The thief cometh not, but for to steal, and to kill, and to destroy: I am come that they might have life, and that they might have it more abundantly."*
> John 10:10

Right here is the separation. The thief (Satan) comes to steal, to kill, and to destroy. He steals from you. He kills your relationship with God. He then destroys your life. Jesus came that we might have abundant life. Anything that steals, kills, and destroys in your life is from Satan. Anything that gives you abundant life is from God. God does not use trials and tribulations to teach you something. He uses the Holy Spirit and the Word of God to teach you something (and if they're not enough for you to learn from, then you're in trouble). Satan uses trials and tribulations to pull the Word of God out of your heart.

> *"Whosoever cometh to me, and heareth my sayings, and doeth them, I will shew you to whom he is like: He is like a man which built an house, and digged deep, and laid the foundation on a rock: and when the flood arose, the stream beat vehemently upon that house, and could not shake it: for it was founded upon a rock. But he that heareth, and doeth not, is like a man that without a foundation built an house upon the earth; against which*

the stream did beat vehemently, and immediately it fell; and the ruin of that house was great."
Luke 6:47-49

Anyone who hears Jesus sayings (the Word of God) and does them, he is like the man who founded his life on the rock. When the trials and storms of life came, he stood through them. When Satan came to attack him, he stood strong on the foundation of the Word of God. He that heard the Word, but did not do it is like the man whose house was destroyed when the trials and storms of life came to him. Notice the storm did not come to teach anybody anything. It came to destroy their houses. Whether your house gets destroyed or not depends on your foundation in the Word of God.

You'll hear about prosperity in the Word of God. Satan first tries to come immediately and steal the Word from you by manmade traditions and other things you've heard. Then he begins his offensive of trials and persecutions. Your washing machine may break and need to be fixed. You may lose your job. You receive an unexpected bill. All of these things are sent to get you off from the Word of God. They're there to get you to believe prosperity isn't for you personally.

He'll have another brother at church discourage you. They'll tell you about how all that prosperity stuff is a load of junk. Someone will make fun of you believing in prosperity while you still have an empty bank account. Someone will accuse you of being "worldly" in wanting to prosper with God. They'll accuse your motives, talk about you behind your back, and some may even not want to associate with you.

No matter what it is you're learning, the same process will take place. You'll learn you are the righteousness of God in Christ Jesus. Satan will use your flesh to get you to sin. You'll sin and he'll immediately bring thoughts about how unworthy you are. He'll tell you that you're not really free from sin. He'll have a dear sister at church ask you who do you think you are? She'll say you're just a worm saved by grace, not the righteousness of God.

You'll be called arrogant. You'll be accused of pride. Don't listen to them. It's all part of Satan's tactics to get the Word of God out of you. He's terrified of that sword you're building. He'll do whatever it takes to steal your Word.

> *"Beloved, think it not strange concerning the fiery trial which is to try you, as though some strange thing happened unto you: But rejoice, inasmuch as ye are partakers of <u>Christ's sufferings</u>; that, when his glory shall be revealed, ye may be glad also with exceeding joy."*
> 1 Peter 4:12-13

Jesus battled the exact same things you're going through. The devil tried to steal the Word of God from him out in the desert. Satan came to tempt him three recorded times and Jesus used the Word on him each time. Then Satan started his war machine up and had all kinds of persecution come against Jesus. They called him a heretic. He said God was His Father and they tried to stone him for it. They constantly plotted against Him to try to take him in His words. The same type of fiery trials will occur to you for the Word's sake.

Satan's Next Strategy is Distraction

> *"And these are they which are sown among thorns; such as hear the word, And the <u>cares of this world</u>, and the <u>deceitfulness of riches</u>, and the <u>lusts of other things</u> entering in, choke the word, and it becometh unfruitful."*
> Mark 4:18-19

The Word has started growing in your life. Those little sprouts are coming out of the ground. Satan is getting nervous. He couldn't steal the Word by manmade traditions. The tribulations and persecutions aren't stopping you. You're staying strong under pressure. The Word of God is about to start producing fruit in your life. He's down to his last shot, so he makes it a big one.

Satan will try to distract you from the Word of God. Let's look at what the Amplified Bible says in this verse.

> *"Then the cares and anxieties of the world and distractions of the age, and the pleasure and delight and false glamour and deceitfulness of riches, and the craving and passionate desire for other things creep in and choke and suffocate the Word, and it becomes fruitless."*
> Mark 4:19, AMP

You've been spending time in the Word of God. You've been studying it daily. It's becoming more real in you every single day. You're living your life based on it. Trials can't stop you. Persecutions can't stop you. Pressure isn't stopping you. So he tries his next tactic, pleasure.

If he can't get you to quit by attacking you, he tries to befriend you. The fiery trials didn't work. So now he wants to make you comfortable. You receive a measure of success. This measure of success provides you with many more opportunities in life for other things. His goal is to so clutter your life that you no longer have time for the Word of God. You no longer have time for prayer.

You may have spent a long time where it seemed like everyone was against you. Now you have all kinds of people for you it seems. You get so busy that your time for the Word of God suffers. Before you couldn't even pay your bills, now you can not only pay them but you can buy yourself some nice things such as a big screen TV and a Jacuzzi. Satan will try to get you so busy doing these other things that you start growing cold for the Word of God and the will of God in your life. You're becoming comfortable.

I fell into this trap for a few years. My wife and I were very poor. We couldn't pay our bills at all. When I started praying for wisdom, things started changing. Satan of course tried to convince me I was wrong because of other things I heard. I went through that step. It was the easiest in my opinion. Next he tried trials and persecutions. Others would tell us how God didn't want to prosper us. It seemed like no one in the world believed me. We'd have times where it would look like we weren't going to make it.

Then Satan threw his most powerful weapon at us. We started becoming successful. I bought TV's, cars, a new home, a spa, and all kinds of other things. I became too busy in my business making money that my Christian life suffered. I never turned my back on him completely, but I grew cold. I never consciously chose to quit seeking God. It just happened. My life and mind became so cluttered with things that I just forgot to seek God. I would put off reading the Bible one day...and then the next...and then the next.

I'd have some responsibility I had to do on Sunday one week. So I'd miss church. It happened again. Then I just didn't feel like going. I wanted time to relax instead. This lasted for a couple of years of my life. It wasn't until I started seeing the "deceitfulness" of riches that I broke out of this rut. The deceitfulness of riches is the thought that riches and things will satisfy you. They won't. They're just an empty shell. That's why you see famous rich people who look like they're on top of the world all of sudden commit suicide. They have everything the world has to offer, and they're still empty inside. They don't see anywhere else to turn.

For me, I got to the place where my business didn't make me happy anymore. Having money and things seemed so empty. I missed being hungry for God. I asked Him to forgive me and renew that hunger in me again. My business had consumed me and I just didn't want a part of that business anymore. So I sold the business and got myself back to the Word of God.

Of all of Satan's tactics, this is the most powerful. He knows God's Word will bring blessings to your life. He knows it will produce fruit. He tried horrible persecution on the early church and the more they were persecuted, the more they multiplied and grew. They fed Christians to the lions for their faith, but they just kept multiplying. So he came up with his most devious tactic of all.

Satan made Christianity socially acceptable. It was promoted as the national religion. The persecution stopped. People became comfortable. They stopped being hungry for and seeking God. Before you were facing possible death just to name the name of Jesus, then you were considered unusual if you didn't believe in Jesus. Christianity as a whole began to die. No one was seeking God, and God's Word started being replaced by man's traditions and other things. We entered the Dark Ages.

The world went through over 1,000 years without any widespread revelation of God before this time. God's Word had been replaced by traditions and dead works which took the place of a real hunger for God. Martin Luther started the Reformation when he received the revelation that the just shall live by faith. The persecution started again as Satan tried to beat the Word of God out of him.

Satan will try each of these tactics on you. He has only one purpose in all of them. It is simply to get the Word of God out of you, because the Word of God is what's dangerous to him. He doesn't care if you live a nice little Christian life as long as you're not walking in the Word of God and setting people free with it.

The Word Produces Fruit in Your Life

"And these are they which are sown on good ground; such as hear the word, and receive it, and bring forth fruit, some <u>thirtyfold</u>, some <u>sixty</u>, and some an <u>hundred</u>."
Mark 4:20

Once you get past the devices of Satan, the Word of God will produce fruit in your life. It may produce a thirtyfold harvest, a sixtyfold harvest, or a hundredfold harvest. God will bless you as much as you let him. Some people will let God bless them just a little bit...thirtyfold. Some will let God bless them twice as much...sixtyfold. A few Christians want it all. They allow God to shower His blessings on them hundredfold.

The hundredfold return stands for receiving everything God has available for you. Think of it as getting 100% of what God has available. Very few Christians ever step up to that point and allow God to do wonders like that in their life. They're usually satisfied with the thirty or the sixty fold returns.

In prosperity we could compare it like this. Some Christians will just receive financial miracles that get them out of trouble when they need them. They never lack, but they are constantly praying to God for another miracle for whatever mess they end up in this time. This would be the thirtyfold blessing.

The next step would be the believer who has enough supply for him and his own. He even has enough to give nice sized offerings at church and to others in need. He doesn't end up in any financial turmoil and he gets to live a happy prosperous life without lack. This would be the sixtyfold level.

Another Christian finds his calling is to generate millions of dollars from his business to help fund numerous Christian works. He works hard, believes God, and walks out his calling on this earth. He generates multiplied millions of dollars. He is able to give millions into the work of the Gospel, and has an overabundance of money constantly available to him for his own life as well. This is the hundredfold return. There are people reading this book right now with that calling. God may be calling you to do this type of work. Generate millions...and fund the Gospel around the world. I'm looking for one million believers like this who go all the way into the hundredfold return in their businesses and their financial lives.

The Deceitfulness of Riches is a Strong Enemy to God's Work

"Then Jesus beholding him loved him, and said unto him, <u>One thing thou lackest</u>: go thy way, sell whatsoever thou hast, and give to the poor, and thou shalt have treasure

in heaven: and come, take up the cross, and follow me. And he was sad at that saying, and went away grieved: for he had great possessions. And Jesus looked round about, and saith unto his disciples, How hardly shall they that have riches enter into the kingdom of God! And the disciples were astonished at his words. But Jesus answereth again, and saith unto them, Children, how hard is it for them that <u>trust in riches</u> to enter into the kingdom of God! It is easier for a camel to go through the eye of a needle, than for a rich man to enter into the kingdom of God. And they were astonished out of measure, saying among themselves, Who then can be saved? And Jesus looking upon them saith, With men it is impossible, but not with God: for with God all things are possible."
Mark 10:21-27

    The rich young man came running to Jesus. He asked Jesus what he needed to do to inherit eternal life. Jesus responded to him that he needed to follow the commandments. The rich young man responded that he has kept the commandments since his youth up. Jesus took a good look at him and loved this young man. This man would make a wonderful disciple. He didn't lie. He didn't steal. He was honest. He loved his neighbor. It put some of the other disciples to shame.

    So Jesus offers him an incredible calling in God's kingdom. He can take up his cross and follow Jesus. He just has to do one act of obedience first. He must give all his possessions to the poor. Then he can come and follow Jesus. The young man went away sorrowful that day. This proves he wanted to do what was right, but the hold his riches had on him were too powerful for him to overcome. They were more important to him than obeying the voice of God.

    Then Jesus goes on to teach about the deceitfulness that is in riches. It is hard for anyone who trusts in riches to enter the kingdom of God. All the disciples were amazed at this. They weren't poor men. There was a tax collector, a doctor, and several men who owned fishing businesses. They were thinking to themselves that this cuts all them out. Who was going to be saved?

Jesus said it was impossible for rich men to be saved in themselves. They couldn't do it. With God, all things are possible though. God can give you the ability to handle wealth. Without him, that wealth will always become a burden to you. You worked to get it, and then you spend the rest of your life fearful about who is going to steal it. Wealth is so powerful it will always rule the life of anyone without God's grace helping them.

Thank God He has given us His grace! His ability is on the inside of us. As long as you keep your eyes open and don't allow the deceitfulness of riches to blind you, God will supply you with the grace and ability you need to handle it. Remember, prosperity destroys a fool (Pro 1:32). You need to pray for God's wisdom and stay in his Word so you never become a fool.

As usual Peter misses the point and he tells Jesus that he has left all to follow him. Then Jesus again tells him about the hundredfold blessing we've been studying.

> *"Then Peter began to say unto him, Lo, we have left all, and have followed thee. And Jesus answered and said, Verily I say unto you, There is no man that hath left house, or brethren, or sisters, or father, or mother, or wife, or children, or lands, for my sake, and the gospel's, But he shall receive an <u>hundredfold</u> now in this time, houses, and brethren, and sisters, and mothers, and children, and lands, with persecutions; and in the world to come eternal life. But many that are first shall be last; and the last first."*
> Mark 10:28-31

Jesus obviously isn't promising they will receive a hundred times as many of these things. They aren't going to get

100 new wives, 100 houses, and 100 lands. He is referring that they are going to get that hundredfold blessing from the parable of the sower. They are going to get everything God has for them since they've given their all to the Gospel.

Rich means, "abundantly supplied." Remember the definition I gave you earlier for rich, "Having more than enough to accomplish my full and complete purpose here on earth." These disciples were receiving the hundredfold blessing. They would receive more than enough to accomplish their full and complete purposes here on earth. They were never going to lack what they needed.

Houses would be available to them. Lands would be available to them. Brethren, sisters, mothers, and children would all be available to them in the family of God. Whatever they needed to accomplish their divine calling and mission would be available to them. Simply put, this is the Father God telling them, "You haven't given up anything. Everything I have is yours."

You haven't given up anything for the Gospel.
Everything the Father has is yours.

Chapter Eight
How to Give God's Way

> *"Therefore I thought it necessary to exhort the brethren, that they would go before unto you, and make up beforehand your bounty, whereof ye had notice before, that the same might be ready, as a <u>matter of bounty</u>, and <u>not as of covetousness</u>. But this I say, He which soweth sparingly shall reap also sparingly; and he which soweth bountifully shall reap also bountifully. Every man according as he <u>purposeth</u> in his heart, so let him give; not <u>grudgingly</u>, or of <u>necessity</u>: for God loveth a <u>cheerful giver</u>."*
> 2 Corinthians 9:5-7

This passage in II Corinthians chapter nine gives us complete instructions on exactly how to give to God. Paul is coming to the Corinthian church to receive an offering. So we actually can learn both sides from this passage, giving offerings and taking up offerings. Paul had sent other Christian brothers ahead of him to Corinth to prepare the gift from the Corinthian church.

The reason he did this was so the gift may be a matter of bounty and not of covetousness. Bounty here is the word, "eulogia" in the Greek and means, "blessing, praise, fine speaking." Covetousness is "pleonexia" and it means, "fraudulency, extortion, greedy desire to have more." Paul wanted the gift the Corinthian church would give to be a matter of praise and blessing, not wrung out of them by extortion and greed. He sent other Christian brothers ahead to collect the offering so none of the Corinthian Christians would feel the offering was being wrung out of them by emotional pitches or greed.

By sending others ahead, this would give the Corinthians time to decide what they should give, and it wouldn't be a quick emotional pitch to get the money out of them. They wouldn't get themselves in trouble by giving more than they could afford, and they also wouldn't miss out on an opportunity to give to God's work because they didn't have enough time to plan. Their giving should be an act of praise and blessing for God's bountiful gifts in our life, not something forced out of them.

Then it goes on to say that those who sow sparingly will also reap sparingly. Those that sow bountifully will also reap bountifully. So don't feel like you have to give, but do remember that those who give out of love will find themselves open to greater blessings God has for their lives. While we have already studied that greed should never be a motivation in our hearts, we can also see from other passages of Scripture that our obedience in giving when the Lord speaks to our heart is vital to our receiving full blessings from him.

"There is that scattereth, and yet increaseth; and there is that withholdeth more than is meet, but it tendeth to poverty. The liberal soul shall be made fat: and he that watereth shall be watered also himself."
Proverbs 11:24-25

"He that hath pity upon the poor lendeth unto the LORD; and that which he hath given will he pay him again."
Proverbs 19:17

"Let him that is taught in the word communicate unto him that teacheth in all good things. Be not deceived; God is not mocked: for whatsoever a man soweth, that shall he also reap. For he that soweth to his flesh shall of the flesh reap corruption; but he that soweth to the Spirit shall of the Spirit reap life everlasting. And let us not be weary in well doing: for in due season we shall reap, if we faint not. As we have therefore opportunity, let us do good unto all men, especially unto them who are of the household of faith."
Galatians 6:6-10

Everyone there was to give as they "purposeth" in their heart. This is the Greek word, "proaireomai" which means, "to choose for oneself before another thing." The believers at Corinth were to choose for themselves how much they would give before the offering would take place. They weren't supposed to make a last minute decision about what they were giving. The decision should have been made beforehand.

This was one of the revelations that really set me free. My wife and I began to pray about any gifts and offerings we would give before we ever went to church. We set a rule for ourselves that we never gave a large gift at church unless we had already decided the gift beforehand. It was never a last minute decision to be made during the offering. When you decide to give during the offering, you can easily be affected by the emotions in the service.

The pastor might have said something you didn't agree with, so you decide to punish him by not giving (the only one who gets punished is you as this is definitely a wrong reason). Or a visiting minister who may not be totally honest could lie about an offering and get you emotionally torn up inside so you give even when God doesn't want you to.

Notice it says we are to decide in our hearts how much to give beforehand. It doesn't say we are to decide with our heads how much to give. Our heads will tell us to figure out what we want to buy and just give some of the extra leftovers. It also doesn't say to listen to anyone else's head. They may tell you that anyone who gives $1,000 will receive an extra blessing from God, but you can only listen to your own heart.

You have to listen to your heart. This means you listen to your conscience and allow the love of God to help you choose how much to give. There may be times where you make sacrifices in your life to give an offering. Remember the widow woman who Jesus said gave more than all of the rich people at the temple (Luke 21:1-4). She sacrificed to make her offering. They simply gave out of their abundance. Love is willing to make sacrifices to help others. So purpose in your heart of love what you will give.

> *"For if there be first a willing mind, it is accepted according to that a man hath, and not according to that he hath not."*
> 2 Corinthians 8:12

The mistake we make sometimes is to think it is the size of the offering that moves God. It isn't. He is not looking at how big or how small the offering is. He isn't calculating the size of your offering to give you a blessing based on its size. He is looking at the attitude and motivation of your heart. If you're truly giving out of love, then that is what He is looking for. If your heart is right, then your offering is accepted.

The Right Attitude for a Giver

> *"Let each one [give] as he has made up his own mind and purposed in his heart, not reluctantly or sorrowfully or under compulsion, for God loves (He takes pleasure in, prizes above other things, and is unwilling to abandon or to do without) a cheerful (joyous, "prompt to do it") giver [whose heart is in his giving]."*
> 2 Corinthians 9:7, AMP

We are to give cheerfully. We are to be joyful about the opportunity to give into God's work. He has already given us access to all things. He has made us rich through taking our place in poverty on the cross. Our giving comes through as thanksgiving and praise for the wonderful work He has already accomplished for us.

Don't give reluctantly. Don't give with a heart full of sorrow over what you're giving. Give with an attitude of gratitude. The Lord owns the whole earth and He has blessed you with prosperity. Even if you don't physically see the prosperity yet, you still have it because Jesus paid the price for you to have it and walk in it. Give him thanks in your offerings.

> *"If ye be willing and obedient, ye shall eat the good of the land:"*
> Isaiah 1:19

It's possible to obey God, and still have the wrong attitude about it. Notice that being obedient isn't enough to eat the good of the land. You also have to be willing. This means you don't sit around complaining or being upset about what you're giving. You do it out of a joyful praise filled heart.

You should also not be giving under compulsion. You shouldn't feel like you have to give and it shouldn't be forced out of you. You shouldn't be giving because of what the pastor, your neighbor, or mother will think of you. You shouldn't be giving because someone makes you feel guilty if you don't give an offering. That missionary's video of the starving kids in Africa may be intended to make you give out of guilt, but you can never allow it to do so (you had better decide how much to give before you get there).

The only correct reason to give is out of a heart filled with love and joy. God doesn't bless you based on the size of your offering. Our life with God is never based on our works. It is based on our love relationship with Him. Be willing to sacrifice things you may want, but do it out of joy for the opportunity to give and help others. That's what giving out of love is all about.

God loves a cheerful giver, but it goes even further than that. God loves everybody. Look at how the Amplified translated the verse. God takes pleasure in a cheerful giver. God prizes above all things a cheerful giver. God is unwilling to abandon or do without a cheerful giver. Maybe you should become a cheerful giver.

God Desires You to Have Abundance in Everything

> *"And God is able to make all grace (every favor and earthly blessing) come to you in abundance, so that you may always and under all circumstances and whatever*

the need be self-sufficient [possessing enough to require no aid or support and furnished in abundance for every good work and charitable donation]. As it is written, He [the benevolent person] scatters abroad; He gives to the poor; His deeds of justice and goodness and kindness and benevolence will go on and endure forever! And [God] Who provides seed for the sower and bread for eating will also provide and multiply your [resources for] sowing and increase the fruits of your righteousness [which manifests itself in active goodness, kindness, and charity]. Thus you will be enriched in all things and in every way, so that you can be generous, and [your generosity as it is] administered by us will bring forth thanksgiving to God."
2 Corinthians 9:8-11, AMP

You will be enriched in all things and in every way. Your gift will cause others to give thanksgiving to God. They will praise God for your gift you gave. More people will experience the love of Christ because of your free gift. For you, you will see God multiply your resources for giving. You will become a funnel. As your finances increase, you give more into the Gospel. As God sees He can trust you with more, you will continually be able to give more and more.

The reason wisdom is so important is because it not only generates the money, but wisdom will also guide you in your use of the money. If you allow the money you make to draw you away from God, you'll lose your peace of mind. That's one good checkup to do on yourself as God prospers you. If you ever get to the place where you constantly fear losing the money, then you've lost your first love which is God and His kingdom.

Religious Gimmicks and Wolves in Sheep's Clothing

"But there were false prophets also among the people, even as there shall be false teachers among you, who

privily shall bring in damnable heresies, even denying the Lord that bought them, and bring upon themselves swift destruction. And many shall follow their pernicious ways; by reason of whom the way of truth shall be evil spoken of. And through <u>covetousness</u> shall they with <u>feigned words make merchandise of you</u>: whose judgment now of a long time lingereth not, and their damnation slumbereth not."
2 Peter 2:1-3

    There are ministers who take up offerings for some far off orphanage. They'll tell you how bad the kids are suffering and how many of them you can feed for just a small offering. Liberal uses of Luke 6:38 will of course occur with great promises of your hundredfold return. They get the audience crying with emotion and filling the offering plates for these poor children. In a few of these cases, there are no children. There is no orphanage. All there is a minister who missed his payment on his Porsche.

    Next week an honest minister (there are way more of these than dishonest ones) comes through to take up an offering for his real orphanage. He only gets a tiny amount of money because he didn't use any emotional tactics and everybody already gave last week. Real children suffer and go hungry, because people allowed emotion to lead them in giving instead of God.

    The last thing I want to give you is the impression that all ministers are running around after your money. They're definitely not. It's that small 1% that ruins the pot and steals the finances. Very few ministers would be willing to get up and lie to their congregations or outright steal their money. It happens, but it is not that frequent. So don't leave this book with a critical spirit believing I told you the ministers are out for your money. I didn't say that. I said there are a few bad apples in the bunch.

    Much more often though a good minister finds himself using some "iffy" methods for raising money. They get themselves into some areas where they probably shouldn't be. They say some things that they probably shouldn't say. They don't do it because they're out to steal from you. They do it because they honestly believe in what they're saying and feel it is best for the work of God they're doing.

Any minister needs to be very careful in the area of fundraising. We can see from the passage we studied that Paul was very careful when he took up the offering from the Corinthians. He wanted them to have time beforehand to seek God for their offering. He didn't want to extort or drag the offering out of them. He wanted them to do it cheerfully from their heart, not from the emotion in their head.

I always get an uneasy feeling when a minister spends an hour taking up an offering. If they spend way more time teaching about why we have to give than other subjects (such as love, wisdom, and faith), it just doesn't sit right with me. Their heart is probably 100% pure before God, but their methods are often wrong. Yes, people need to be taught to give. Every church needs teaching on offerings and how to give offerings correctly. What they don't need is exhortations of give, give, give without everything else we're learning here.

They would be much better off following Paul's example of teaching about offerings. Then take up the offering at a later date just as he did. So they may take the normal offering Monday. Then do a full teaching about giving. Then take up the next offering on Tuesday, not right after they do the teaching. This would give people time to give from their hearts, not from their heads.

There is no problem at all telling people how the money will be used and even reading testimonials from people who have been helped. That is all fine. We see Paul talking about the purposes of money he takes up also. The problem only occurs when it is used to draw on the emotions of people to pull a larger offering than God would really want them to give.

Using wrong methods in taking up offerings can turn people off to the Gospel. Using wild claims of multiplied returns or begging for money is often found on opposite ends of the spectrum, but they are both problems in this area. You'll hear TV or radio ministers sometimes say, "If you don't give, we're going off the air." Well, go off the air then. If God can't take care of you, you're in trouble anyway. I'm definitely not going to get in His way and keep you on the air.

All of these methods can turn people off to the Gospel. Our goal as Christian believers is to get as many people as possible into the kingdom. We need money to do that so do take up offerings. Do tell people what it is for. Do tell them how it has helped people. Just don't turn it into an emotional party trying to force people to give out of greed, guilt, or fear.

Don't Fall for the Old Blessed Item Scam

In the Dark Ages churches would often sell splinters from the cross, saint's bones, and blessed gold coins held by the master Himself. If you wanted to be saved, you simply bought whatever it was they were selling and you'd be blessed of God. Martin Luther received the revelation that the just shall live by faith. They didn't live by works nor by the religious artifacts they purchased. He spoke out against the abuses in the church and started the Reformation.

You would think we'd be past that point in the church, but we're not. You still see this kind of thing going on. You can go to churches where they sell blessed wallets that will never run out of money. They sell blankets that have been prayed over for your babies. They sell specially anointed communion sets. They sell holy water from the Jordan River.

None of these are any different from the artifacts being sold during the Dark Ages. Sometimes people will use the scripture where handkerchiefs are taken from Paul's body and used to heal the sick (Acts 19:12). Notice that Paul wasn't charging for these though! Go buy your own blanket at Wal-Mart and ask an anointed minister to pray over it, but don't fall for the religious item scam.

Name Your Seed

There is a teaching circulating that you should "Name Your Seed" when you give an offering. When you give something, they tell you to expect God to give you a specific blessing that you name off. By this teaching, when you give your offering you may tell God you're believing for a house.

You're in danger of getting into a works mentality when you do something like that. You could never go down to the altar and tell God you're getting saved based on the good works you did last week. You couldn't tell God to heal you based on the fact you prayed for 100 sick people this week. God's grace doesn't come that way. Grace is grace. It is unmerited, unearned favor. God gives to you because He loves you. He answers your prayers because you're His child.

"Therefore I say unto you, What things soever ye desire, when ye pray, believe that ye receive them, and ye shall have them."
Mark 11:24

He says to believe you receive when you pray...not when you give an offering. In fact, there is nothing found around this verse that talks about giving at all. You will find the next verse talks about forgiveness. Unforgiveness will keep you from receiving the answers to prayer, but we don't see anything about giving or naming a seed when you pray.

You believe you receive something when you pray. God gives it to you by His grace. Yes, you need to be a giver, but you're not giving to try and get God to answer your prayers. You are an obedient child of God who gives out of a heart full of love and joy. You are not a servant working for a paycheck (the new house in this example). You're a son with free access to all the Father's resources.

Special Money Multiplying Anointing

Sometimes a minister will claim God has given them a special anointing for prosperity. They'll say that if you send an offering to them, you'll be blessed by God in your finances. They'll claim a special anointing that money sent to them is multiplied more than money you send to other ministers or give to the poor. This is definitely in error.

Notice that when the rich young man came to Jesus to find out how to be perfect, Jesus told him to sell everything he had and give it to the poor. He didn't say sell everything you have and give it to me. Nobody is more anointed than Jesus, yet he told the young man to give to the poor. There wasn't any special anointing for giving to Jesus. There isn't any special anointing to give to any specific minister.

If you were to ask an honest minister to pray for you to get out of debt, he wouldn't tell you have to give him a big offering. He would pray for you to receive wisdom, for God to show you every area you've been acting foolishly in, and for you to receive new ideas and business plans. That's how you get out of debt. It is not by a special gifted anointing that just miraculously gets you out of debt.

Let's settle this here. You will not be blessed more for giving to certain ministries. You will not be blessed more because you gave in a special offering. You will definitely not be blessed more for giving a specific amount the minister claims is anointed. God already desires to bless and has already blessed you with all blessings through Jesus.

Your goal in giving is to give out of love. Give because you honestly care about people. You care about people coming to Jesus and you care about their daily needs. Partner up with a ministry which is accomplishing goals that are dear to your heart. Give to every good work, but don't believe some of the scams people use to pull money out of you.

Chapter Nine
Tithing...By Law or By Grace

"Will a man rob God? Yet ye have robbed me. But ye say, Wherein have we robbed thee? In tithes and offerings. <u>Ye are cursed with a curse</u>: for ye have robbed me, even this whole nation. Bring ye all the tithes into the storehouse, that there may be meat in mine house, and prove me now herewith, saith the LORD of hosts, if I will not open you the windows of heaven, and pour you out a blessing, that there shall not be room enough to receive it. And I will rebuke the devourer for your sakes, and he shall not destroy the fruits of your ground; neither shall your vine cast her fruit before the time in the field, saith the LORD of hosts. And all nations shall call you blessed: for ye shall be a delightsome land, saith the LORD of hosts."
Malachi 3:8-12

The scripture above is one of the most used scriptures in the Bible in regards to tithing. Under the Old Covenant, people were cursed with a curse if they didn't tithe. If they weren't paying their tithes, they were robbing God. The devourer (Satan) would then be allowed to destroy the fruits of their labor and their ground. Their ability to produce would be cut off. If they did produce an income, it would be consumed by something else.

Tithing simply means 10%. The people were ordered by the Law to give 10% of all their income. This was part of the Law and it carried both blessings and a curse just like everything else in the Law. You can go to Deuteronomy 28 to read all the blessings and curses of the Law. If you followed the Law, you were blessed. If you broke the Law, you would be cursed. This is what we see happening in Malachi 3:8-12. They were being cursed with a curse because they chose to break the Law of God.

> "*Christ hath redeemed us from the curse of the law, being made a curse for us: for it is written, Cursed is every one that hangeth on a tree:*"
> Galatians 3:13

Jesus came to the earth, fulfilled all the Law, and then gave Himself in our place by taking the curse of the Law upon Himself. We have been redeemed from the curse of the Law. He took our place in the curse and suffered all the curses and judgment of God that we deserved. We are now free from the curse of the Law. It holds no more power over us.

So believers are not cursed with a curse if they don't tithe. Jesus already took and paid the price for that curse. All the preaching that has been preached about tithing with the intention of scaring believers into tithing is wrong. You don't have to be afraid your Father will curse you for not giving to Him. He won't curse you ever. You're in Christ, and Jesus has suffered all the curse you ever had coming to you.

Old Covenant Versus New Covenant

> "*But now hath he obtained a more excellent ministry, by how much also he is the mediator of a better covenant, which was established upon better promises. For if that first covenant had been faultless, then should no place have been sought for the second. For finding fault with them, he saith, Behold, the days come, saith the Lord, when I will make a new covenant with the house of Israel and with the house of Judah:*"
> Hebrews 8:6-8, KJV

Jesus was the mediator of a new and better covenant. The law was simply a schoolmaster to bring us to Christ (Galatians 3:24). The entire Law was fulfilled in Jesus as He walked the earth. He walked as a perfect man under the Law. He was the only righteous man. Then when He took on our nature on the cross, He gave us His righteous standing with God. You have His righteousness if you believe in Him. That means all the blessings of the Old Covenant are yours by faith simply because you are in Christ. It is not because of anything you have done. No one can be justified based on their works (Galatians 2:16).

In the Old Covenant, you were financially blessed because you followed the works of the Law. If you paid all your tithes (there was actually more than one tithe when you study it out) and gave to the poor, you were blessed by the Law. In the New Covenant, Jesus has fulfilled all righteousness for you…and it is simply yours by faith.

In the Old Covenant, your blessings were based on your works. In the New Covenant, the blessings are already yours by faith through Jesus. He completed the works of the Law for you. You are free from the Law. We are no longer under the sacrifices of the Old Covenant. We are no longer under the Sabbath of the Old Covenant. We are no longer under the food laws of the Old Covenant. We are no longer under the tithe of the Old Covenant.

We are in the New Covenant of grace. Every blessing is received from God by grace through faith. We are no longer under any of the Old Testament Law. We are to serve God out of a new heart with new motives. The one rule of the New Covenant is to walk in love. Love is to motivate our actions toward God, our actions toward man, and all of our giving. We are no longer under the Old Covenant Law. We are in New Covenant love.

Instructions for the Gentile Believers

"Forasmuch as we have heard, that certain which went out from us have troubled you with words, subverting your souls, saying, <u>Ye must be circumcised, and keep the law: to whom we gave no such commandment</u>: It seemed

> *good unto us, being assembled with one accord, to send chosen men unto you with our beloved Barnabas and Paul, Men that have hazarded their lives for the name of our Lord Jesus Christ. We have sent therefore Judas and Silas, who shall also tell you the same things by mouth. <u>For it seemed good to the Holy Ghost, and to us, to lay upon you no greater burden</u> than these necessary things; That ye abstain from meats offered to idols, and from blood, and from things strangled, and from fornication: from which <u>if ye keep yourselves, ye shall do well.</u> Fare ye well."*
> Acts 15:24-29

Certain Jewish believers went into the Gentile church and told them that they must be circumcised and keep all the Law. Unless they did this, they couldn't be saved. The church at Jerusalem met together and decided to lay no greater burden on the new believers than that which they consider vital to their salvation. They told them they did not have to be circumcised nor keep the Law of Moses. They gave them only a few "rules"...

1. Abstain from meats offered to idols.
2. Abstain from blood.
3. Abstain from things strangled.
4. Abstain from fornication.

They gave them NO other rules. Not only that, but they told the new Gentile believers they were doing good if they simply followed those rules. Notice that it wasn't just the church that decided on this. The Jews said it "seemed good to the Holy Ghost." These were the Holy Spirit's instructions for the new believers. They were not to be given the burden of the Law...including tithing.

I've seen some churches in our day that hand out papers to new believers about all the "laws" they now have to keep. They get a new baby Christian in and then bind them with the Law.

Some churches don't even allow anyone to be a "member" unless they commit to legalistic tithing. These churches obviously never read Acts chapter fifteen.

Notice that the apostles (and the Holy Spirit) didn't even command the new believers to follow all the moral law such as honoring your parents, not lying, and not committing murder. Why is that? It's because we have one commandment in the New Covenant...and it's written on our hearts...LOVE. If you love your parents, you will honor them. If you love someone, you will not lie to them or murder them.

The apostles knew that the new Gentile believers had received the same Holy Spirit they had. They knew every believer could have a personal relationship with God. They knew they didn't have to teach all the moral law to the new believers, because the Holy Spirit would train them (Hebrews 8:11). You won't be able to walk in a close fellowship with God and keep right on lying, stealing, or murdering. You also won't be able to develop that close fellowship and stay greedy. You will become a giver by love without being legalistically commanded to do so by Old Testament law.

Judaizers and the Book of Galatians

Paul continually had a problem with the Judaizers. They followed him around and tried to bring Paul's new Gentile believers under the Law wherever he went. For them, circumcision is one of the laws they focused on the most. They continually told all the new believers they had to be circumcised. Paul fought this doctrine with all his heart...even calling it "another" gospel (Galatians 1:6) and saying Christ would profit them nothing (Galatians 5:2).

The entire book of Galatians is about this subject. I suggest you go read all six chapters before you even finish reading this chapter. The Judaizers were turning the Gentile believers away from Christ and back into the law. Circumcision was the key issue they focused on. We still have Judaizers in our day, but instead of circumcision, they focus on tithing. I have yet to see any church with an usher checking to make sure members are circumcised when they come in (and I hope I never do)…but I have seen them not allowing any member who didn't tithe.

> *"Wherefore thou art no more a servant, but a son; and if a son, then an heir of God through Christ. Howbeit then, when ye knew not God, ye did service unto them which by nature are no gods. But now, after that ye have known God, or rather are known of God, <u>how turn ye again to the weak and beggarly elements</u>, whereunto ye desire again to be in bondage? Ye observe days, and months, and times, and years."*
> Galatians 4:7-10, KJV

Paul asks the Galatians why they desire to be in bondage again. You used to be in bondage to your own sinful nature and to idols in the world. Why are you allowing yourself to be put back into bondage of the Law? Paul calls these things weak and beggarly elements. Why would you want to go back into the law which had no power to make anyone perfect before God (Hebrews 7:19)?

In the New Covenant, we are not just servants like they were in the Old Covenant. We are sons and heirs of God through Jesus Christ. Everything the Father has is ours by faith in His grace. It is not by Law. God does not treat us as servants anymore. He treats us as sons. Yet, many believers are being taught to walk in the financial realm like Old Covenant servants. If you're going to walk in God's full measure of grace, you'll have to understand it is all by grace…and not by law.

> *"For <u>as many as are of the works of the law are under the curse</u>: for it is written, Cursed is every one that continueth not in all things which are written in the book of the law to do them."*
> Galatians 3:10, KJV

> *"And all who depend on the Law [who are seeking to be justified by obedience to the Law of rituals] <u>are under a curse and doomed to disappointment and destruction</u>, for it is written in the Scriptures, Cursed (accursed, devoted to destruction, doomed to eternal punishment) be everyone who does not continue to abide (live and remain) by all the precepts and commands written in the Book of the Law and to practice them. [Deut 27:26.]"*
> Galatians 3:10, AMP

Galatians 3:10 says that all those who depend upon the law are under a curse. They're doomed to disappointment and destruction. Is it any wonder why we have so much poverty in the church...even to those who believe in prosperity? Instead of walking in faith by grace, most believers have been bound to the Law and to works. God is merciful and blesses us all He can, but He is limited by many believers who put their own finances under a curse. Instead of giving out of their heart in a motive of love, they are giving out of greed or fear based on Law.

Scriptures Taken Out of Context to Prove Tithing

Ministers who preach tithing focus on three primary verses to teach tithing (all taken out of context). The verses they use are Malachi 3:8-12, Luke 11:42, and Genesis 14:19-20. Let's cover each of those scriptures quickly so there isn't any confusion on this subject.

The first and most popular scripture for tithing is Malachi 3:8-12 and it is the basis of every message I have ever heard preached on tithing. There is no New Testament teaching on tithing (since it was not taught in the New Covenant), so ministers must use an Old Covenant passage as their base text. It says that the Old Testament believers were robbing God and were cursed because they did not tithe. There were many curses for failing to keep the Law, and they were under these curses since they did not tithe.

We are in a New Covenant and Jesus has taken the curse of the law for us (Galatians 3:13). Satan has already been defeated for our sakes at the cross (Colossians 2:15). A big problem in the church world is that ministers often teach the Old Testament without bringing it through the cross. All scripture is good for our training (II Timothy 3:16), but many scriptures relate to us differently in the New Covenant.

That's why the basis for our teaching and study should be in the New Testament epistles. You need to have a very strong foundation in the New Covenant before you spend too much time studying out of the Old Covenant. Even when you study the Gospels (Matthew, Mark, Luke, and John), you have to remember that the Old Covenant was still in force. The New Covenant did not start until Jesus fulfilled all the Old Covenant at His cross and resurrection.

So the promises and curses in Malachi 3 are no longer about tithing for New Covenant Christians, since tithing is Old Covenant Law. Those promises would be based on faith in Jesus...and the righteousness He has provided you with at the cross. He took the curse there for you, and then provided you with His righteous standing and the blessing of the chapter. It is simply up to you to believe in His grace.

Let's take a look at scripture number two of the tithing teachers...

> "But woe unto you, <u>Pharisees</u>! for ye tithe mint and rue and all manner of herbs, and pass over judgment and the love of God: these ought ye to have done, and not to leave the other undone."
> Luke 11:42, KJV

Ministers sometimes use Luke 11:42 to tell us that Jesus encouraged us to tithe. Jesus told the Pharisees they needed judgement and the love of God...and not to leave tithing undone. The tithing teachers say Jesus is telling us we should all tithe. That is not what He said.

First of all, look at who Jesus is talking to in this verse. He is talking to the Pharisees...Jews who are still under the Old Covenant (Jesus had not died yet to create the New Covenant). They were still under the Law so they should have been tithing. So of course Jesus told them to keep tithing. While Jesus walked the earth, the Old Covenant was still in effect. Men were still under the Law and unrighteous before God. It wasn't until Jesus took our place on the cross and rose again that the Covenants changed. After Jesus' death and resurrection, there was never an instruction to tithe. We were only given instructions to give according to our hearts (II Corinthians 9:7).

Let's go to the third scripture used to teach tithing...

"And he blessed him, and said, Blessed be Abram of the most high God, possessor of heaven and earth: And blessed be the most high God, which hath delivered thine enemies into thy hand. And he gave him tithes of all." Genesis 14:19-20

This story about Abraham is also quoted in Hebrews 7:4-9. The tithing teaching from this passage is that since Abraham gave a tithe 400 years before the Law, then tithing must not simply be under the Law. There are three huge holes in this teaching which are never mentioned. The first hole is that no one commanded Abraham to tithe. He did it simply because he chose to, not because he was ordered to. Giving 10% of your income away is a good practice, but it should be from your heart and out of faith...not because of law.

The second hole is that this is the ONLY time we have any record of Abraham tithing. It doesn't say it was a habit of Abraham or a way of life. It is the only time Melchizedek is ever mentioned. This time is the only time we know Abraham gave 10%...and it was out of the spoils from this one battle. This passage does not say he tithed all of his earnings throughout his life as the tithing teachers use this passage to try to prove.

The third hole is that Abraham was commanded to be circumcised by God along with his whole household (Genesis

17:10). So if Abraham is an example of tithing, he is also our example of circumcision. Yet, Paul wrote the entire book of Galatians on the issue of legalism and especially circumcision. The Judaizers would have been using Abraham as proof that circumcision was required…and today they use Abraham as a proof text that tithing is required. It's the same legalistic teaching in a different package.

How to Give Under Grace

> *"For, brethren, ye have been called unto liberty; only <u>use not liberty for an occasion to the flesh</u>, but by love serve one another."*
> Galatians 5:13

We are no longer under the Law including tithing. Does this mean we shouldn't give to our local churches? Of course not! We are called to liberty and freedom, but we cannot use that freedom to pleasure our flesh. Our freedom should be used to serve one another in love. Love is our one standard and requirement as New Testament believers.

I had to overcome a lot of fear to write this chapter. First of all, I had to overcome the fear of rejection. I know there may be some ministers who won't take this chapter nicely. The doctrine of tithing has been so ingrained in us that it's very difficult to get free from. My second fear was that some people would use our "liberty" in Christ just to please their own flesh. There are teachers out there who teach against tithing just so they can keep more money for themselves.

Our motive in every part of our Christian life must be love. So our freedom from the Law and tithing is not so you can just keep more for yourself. It's so you can be free from fear and works. You are to give as you purpose in your heart. Giving 10% is a good place to start. If you're able, you could give 20%, 30%, or even 50%. I know of businessmen who give 90% of their net income. Learning this truth about tithing and New Testament giving will not cause you to give less if your heart is right. You'll want to give more out of a thankful heart for God's wonderful grace and love for you.

Let's take a look at one example of New Testament giving...

> *"Neither was there any among them that lacked: for as many as were possessors of lands or houses sold them, and brought the prices of the things that were sold,"*
> Acts 4:34

They went well beyond any Law of tithing. They didn't just give 10%. They gave ALL the money from what they sold. They weren't giving because they had to. They were giving because they were in love with Jesus and in love with people. God has given us the same spirit of love in our hearts. We just need to learn to yield to it. We should be giving as the Lord leads us in every good work (Galatians 6:10).

If you're tithing right now, should you stop? Of course not! These believers didn't stop at just 10%. They gave their all. Saving and giving 10% of your money is a good practice. This chapter hasn't been written to make you give less! Having a set percentage such as 10% is a good way to discipline yourself and your spending. So keep giving 10%, but do it out of faith and love. Your ability and desire to give will increase once you start doing it out of love...and learn to walk in His wisdom.

Don't tithe because of legalism and fear of what will happen if you don't. Don't tell God He has to bless you because of how righteous you are in your tithing! Tell God from now on you're giving out of love for Him and His work. You accept His grace and His blessings on you, and you want to learn to be a giver His way. If you act in faith, He will prosper you and He'll increase your ability to give so you can give even more.

I used to give because I was trying to get rich.
Now I give because I know I already am rich through Jesus.

Chapter Ten
Waiting For a Miracle And Missing Your Blessing

"But thou shalt remember the LORD thy God: for it is he that <u>giveth thee power to get wealth</u>, that he may establish his covenant which he sware unto thy fathers, as it is this day."
Deuteronomy 8:18

God's best for you is not a miracle. He wants you to become a miracle worker. His best for you is to walk in His full blessings and be the one who provides miracles for others. Way too often the blessing of God is walking right by us as we sit there waiting for a miracle.

Pay careful attention to the scripture above. It says God gives us the power to get wealth. It does not say God gives us the wealth. It says He gives us the power to get it ourselves. There is quite a bit of difference between giving you something outright and giving you the power to get it. Giving you the wealth means Jesus knocks on your door and hands you a check for a million dollars. Giving you the power to get wealth means Jesus gives you the wisdom, knowledge, and ability to go out and make a million dollars. See the difference?

When my wife and I were broke and in debt, we were praying for a financial miracle. We were expecting someday someone would walk up to us and give us a check to get us out of all our problems. We gave offerings expecting a hundredfold return with that miracle check in mind. We even named that as our seed. We'd say we're giving an offering for that check.

We both continued to work odd jobs just waiting for the day when the miracle check would come. I would sit there and imagine it. We confessed it. We bound the devil. We did everything we had been taught to do, but the miracle check never came.

I've already told you about the revelation that changed my life...to pray for wisdom daily instead of praying for money. God would have had to break His own Word to drop that miracle check in my lap. There were areas of my finances that were dramatically opposed to the Word.

As soon as I would have received the money, I would have begun the process of getting back into debt. Within a year I would have been praying for another large financial miracle. That process would have been a never-ending cycle. I'd get in trouble and go to God to get me out again...and again...and again...and the whole time it would have been because of my own foolishness.

> *"For the turning away of the simple shall slay them, and the <u>prosperity of fools shall destroy them</u>."*
> Proverbs 1:32

If a fool finds a way to be prosperous, their prosperity will destroy them. No matter how high they go in life, their foolishness will find a way to knock them back down again. Take two foolish people. One may be making $10,000 a year and the other one may be making $100,000 a year. If they're both severely foolish with their spending, then we'll soon see both of them up to their necks in debt. At this point, the $100,000 a year guy probably has more junk, but he is also a lot further in debt. The $10,000 a year person may owe $50,000. The $100,000 person may owe $500,000. They were both fools with their money and they are both in the same situation now.

Someone wins the lottery and gets paid $1,000,000. Go back and check on their life in 5 years and you'll find them flat broke again the majority of the time. They spent all their money and in many cases may actually owe more money than they did when they started. That big check eventually put them in worse shape than when they started.

Why does this happen? It's because their mindset never changed. They never learned wisdom. They got the big check, but they were still just as big of a fool as they were when they were broke. So the Word of God eventually took effect in their life and their foolishness destroyed them. This is a basic principle in God's Word. Foolishness will keep you poor. If a fool does somehow get or inherit wealth, he'll lose it or he'll eventually end up so in bondage to it that it destroys the rest of his life.

People hear about prosperity and give away every penny they have. If you do that, tonight may be a cold hungry night. Other people have written a "faith check" as they call it. They don't have the money in the bank when they write the check, but they claim God will put it in there for them before it is needed. That is foolishness. You are making a legal statement that you have the money in the bank when you write the check. They can put you in jail for check fraud.

Sometimes people quit their job and claim they're going to live by faith. They quote scriptures such as God saying He will supply all your needs, but they ignore the ones that say if you don't work, you don't eat. Then they mooch off others to survive. If someone doesn't give something to them, they'll claim they're not walking in love. They need to be shown some tough love. Before you feed them or give them anything, hand them a broom to sweep the floor.

Don't Be Flakey

"If we have sown unto you spiritual things, <u>is it a great thing if we shall reap your carnal things</u>? If others be partakers of this power over you, are not we rather? Nevertheless we have not used this power; but suffer all things, lest we should hinder the gospel of Christ. Do ye not know that they which minister about holy things live of the things of the temple? and they which wait at the altar are partakers with the altar? Even so hath the Lord

ordained <u>that they which preach the gospel should live of the gospel.</u>"
1 Corinthians 9:11-14

Where do we get some of our ideas? We get them by misapplying certain scriptures and also by the testimonials we here from others. For example, why did I expect God to send me a big check someday? I believed it because many ministers have talked about how they received the miracle check that got them out of debt, that bought them a house, or other things. Praise God for them! The problem is that we expect God has to do things the same way for us. He doesn't. He is no respecter of persons, so what He does for one, He will do for all. He does NOT use the same methods to do it all the time.

God has ordained that preachers of the Gospel should live of the Gospel. So preachers take offerings to support them in their ministry. They spend their time teaching, preaching, counseling, studying, praying, and sharing what the Lord shares with them. God may have them pastor in one set location or He may have them evangelize around the world. Either way, He has ordained that offerings be given to them to support their ministry and for their daily living. They may minister in one place and get a small offering that doesn't meet their budget. At the next place they go they may get a bigger offering that makes up for the lower one. God may send someone to give them a special gift for them or their ministry.

They are called to be supported by the body of Christ. You may not be called to a full-time ministry like that. The majority of the body of Christ isn't called to do it full-time. Every member of the body has a ministry. The majority are called to function as a worker in the marketplace for their living. Even the great apostle Paul was a tentmaker to support himself in the ministry. So if anyone ever looks down on you for being a part-time minister, tell them if it's good enough for Paul, it's good enough for you.

The main way God supplies full-time ministers is through money given to them by the body of Christ. The main way God will supply the majority of the body of Christ is through their jobs, their businesses, and their investments. God may have someone come and hand you a check someday, but that is not His best plan for you. And you definitely should never try to limit God to just giving you a check. He can do so much more for you than that kind of limited thinking allows.

**God doesn't just want to hand you a check.
God wants to bless your job, your business, and your investments.**

Christians who are always looking for the miracle check will miss the many blessings God has for them. God desires to provide you with divine favor and blessings every day. If you ignore those opportunities and keep looking out there somewhere for the check, you'll miss out on what He has for you.

You can be blessed in a multitude of ways...

1. You get promoted at work.
2. You get a pay raise.
3. A different company hires you for more money.
4. You work on commissions and your sales double.
5. You get a bonus at work for finding a new way for them to profit.
6. Your business gets a grant.
7. Your business gets free publicity.
8. You decide to change your advertising and you triple your customers.
9. You come up with two brand new ways to make additional profits.
10. Your company gets bought out by a larger company for a big sum.
11. You find a way to reduce waste and costs by 25%.
12. You hire a new salesman who can sell like crazy.
13. You buy a piece of real estate and it doubles in value.
14. You buy a house for a fraction of the cost and fix it up.

15. You sense God's leading in a stock and triple your money.
16. You go to a garage sale and find a painting worth $10,000 for $5.
17. The new furniture you wanted is put on clearance for half price.
18. You are given a new car for guessing the number of jellybeans.
19. And this list could go on forever...

That list could be virtually endless. There are so many ways God can bless you and give you favor. The majority of the above just don't look like miracles, so people skip right over them. They're waiting for something spectacular to happen. They're waiting to find a bag of money or for money to rain on them out of heaven.

The reason people miss so many opportunities in life is because most opportunities come disguised as work. Notice most of the items in my list above include some kind of work along with them. They include you doing something. This is because God wants a family business. He is the brains of the operation, but you work alongside him. Don't get the idea He works for you as your employee. You're a team, and He's the one in charge of the team.

Pray for Wisdom Right Now

"If any of you lack wisdom, let him ask of God, that giveth to all men liberally, and upbraideth not; and it shall be given him. But let him ask in faith, nothing wavering. For he that wavereth is like a wave of the sea driven with the wind and tossed. For let not that man think that he shall receive any thing of the Lord. A double minded man is unstable in all his ways."
James 1:5-8

If you lack wisdom (and you probably do), then ask for wisdom from God. He will give you His wisdom liberally and will not hold back. The wisdom you're requesting will be given to you as long as you ask in faith. You have to truly believe God will give you wisdom. He says He does. Is He able to give you wisdom? Most definitely He is. Are you able to receive wisdom? God says you can.

So ask, and believe you're receiving His wisdom. You might have been a blockhead yesterday, but you're going to pray for His wisdom to change today. Begin praying for wisdom everyday of your life. Pray something simply like the below prayer.

"Dear Father, please give me wisdom today. Teach me how to think, speak, and act correctly. Keep my eyes open for opportunities to be blessed and to bless other people. Show me how to succeed today and how to do the best job I possibly can in everything I do. Reveal any of the foolish things I've been doing in my life to block your blessings. Teach me how every area of the Word of God applies to my daily life today. Open my ears to hear your voice today and give me the strength to obey when you speak. Thank you Father for your wisdom, your blessings, and your divine favor on me today."

Don't pray that prayer unless you expect God to answer it. If you believe it when you pray, you're going to start seeing some things you haven't seen before. You're going to see some of the foolish things you're doing. You're going to see areas of your life you haven't submitted to Him yet. Be glad and praise God for it, because He'll start changing you everyday from now on if you're serious about that prayer.

Your friends might not even recognize you as the same person anymore. When the Spirit of God came upon Saul in the Old Testament, it said he was changed into another man.

"And the Spirit of the LORD will come upon thee, and thou shalt prophesy with them, and <u>shalt be turned into another man</u>."
1 Samuel 10:6

Chapter Eleven
The Grasshopper Complex

"And Caleb stilled the people before Moses, and said, Let us go up at once, and possess it; for we are well able to overcome it. But the men that went up with him said, <u>We be not able</u> to go up against the people; for they are stronger than we. And they brought up <u>an evil report</u> of the land which they had searched unto the children of Israel, saying, The land, through which we have gone to search it, is a land that eateth up the inhabitants thereof; and all the people that we saw in it are men of a great stature. And there we saw the giants, the sons of Anak, which come of the giants: and <u>we were in our own sight as grasshoppers, and so we were in their sight.</u>"
Numbers 13:30-33

When you pray for wisdom, you must believe you receive it. If you doubt God has given it to you, then you're just like the seas which are tossed to and fro by every wind. You believe God has given you wisdom when you hear a great faith building message. Then a friend comes along and says they aren't too sure about it, and you doubt. You hear another good message and you're on top of the wave. You do something dumb and you then call yourself stupid. You just sunk your own boat.

You're acting way too much like the children of Israel did out in the wilderness after God delivered them from Egypt. They would see a mighty miracle of God, and they would praise Him for His mighty works. They would get hungry and complain it was better for them back in Egypt. God would bless them and they would praise Him. They'd get thirsty and complain things were better back in Egypt.

Moses went up into the mountain with God for 40 days and the people of Israel made a golden calf to bow down and worship. It had been just over a month since they had seen His mighty miracles and they forgot about Him. They were ready and willing to bow down to a false God when the real God was visible up on the mountainside only a little time before. That is called wavering and it is what God doesn't want you to do when you pray for wisdom in James chapter one.

Caleb was full of faith in God and said, "Let's go right now and take the land, for we can do it!" Caleb believed God when He told them they were going to take this land. He had faith in the Word of God. He remembered how the Egyptian army was one of the mightiest armies on earth and God destroyed them without even a fight. The size of their enemies didn't matter, because God is bigger than anything they could face.

The other spies disagreed with Caleb. They said, "We be not able." They said they couldn't do it. The people in the land were too strong for them. The men are too big they said. It was their promised land and it was a great land, but the giants were too big for them. The most telling statement they made was this one, "We were in our own sight as grasshoppers, and so we were in their sight." They saw themselves as insignificant, and others saw them the same way.

Notice God called this an evil report of the land. Unbelief in God's Word is evil. Believing you are less than what God has said you are is evil. Believing the giants standing in your way can stop you is evil. All unbelief is sin (Rom 14:23). They were full of fear and unbelief, and the big pity-party started.

> *"And _all the congregation lifted up their voice, and cried;_ and the people wept that night. And all the children of Israel murmured against Moses and against Aaron: and the whole congregation said unto them, Would God that we had died in the land of Egypt! or _would God we had died in this wilderness!"_*
> Numbers 14:1-2

The Grasshopper Complex

I wouldn't have wanted to be in the congregation that night. There were over a million Israelites and it says they all lifted up their voices, cried, and wept that night. It would have been a noisy place with Kleenex everywhere. They bawled. They cried. They wept. They had the biggest pity-party of all time. I've seen some pity-parties before, but never one with a million plus people participating. It would have been a sight. They all cried out and wished they had died in Egypt or the wilderness.

> "Say unto them, As truly as I live, saith the LORD, <u>as ye have spoken in mine ears, so will I do to you</u>: <u>Your carcases shall fall in this wilderness</u>; and all that were numbered of you, according to your whole number, from twenty years old and upward, which have murmured against me,"
> Numbers 14:28-29

When you skip to the end of the chapter, you see God saying He will answer their prayers that night. As they had spoken, He would do to them. All of those people were to die in the wilderness just like they said. Was it God's perfect will for the people to wander around in the wilderness and die in the wilderness? No. His perfect will would have been for them to obey Him and go into the Promised Land right then. The people chose to take a 40 year detour through the wilderness to die first.

There is a doctrine running around in the church today that God puts us through a wilderness experience to test us and prepare us for where we're going. Whenever you see most of the people who believe this doctrine, they have a long face. They tell you about the wilderness they're going through. They tell you about the test and trial they're experiencing. They're just wandering around in the wilderness.

Quit wandering around in the wilderness. God didn't send the Israelites to the wilderness to perfect them. He didn't send them there to train them. He sent them there to get rid of them so He could raise up new believers (if Moses wouldn't have prayed, God would have killed the whole bunch of them immediately right there). They went to the wilderness because of their unbelief. God's will was for them to enter the Promised Land and take it right then! THEY chose to spend 40 years in the wilderness to die. They decided that dying in the wilderness was easier than running the giants out of their promised land.

> *"Surely they shall not see the land which I sware unto their fathers, neither shall any of them that provoked me see it: But my servant Caleb, <u>because he had another spirit with him</u>, and hath followed me fully, him will I bring into the land whereinto he went; and his seed shall possess it."*
> Numbers 14:23-24

> *"But <u>without faith it is impossible to please him</u>: for he that cometh to God must believe that he is, and that <u>he is a rewarder</u> of them that diligently seek him."*
> Hebrews 11:6

Caleb had another spirit with him. He wasn't full of the spirit of fear. He wasn't full of unbelief. He believed God's Word. He believed they would take the Promised Land just like God said. Without faith it is impossible to please God. The Israelites didn't please God. Caleb pleased God and was rewarded for it. Caleb and Joshua were the only ones older than 20 who entered into the Promised Land.

They Were Bound By The Grasshopper Complex

> *"When Pharaoh let the people go, God led them not by way of the land of the Philistines, although that was nearer; for God said, Lest the people <u>change their purpose when they see war and return to Egypt</u>. But God led the people around by way of the wilderness toward the Red Sea. And the Israelites went up marshaled [in ranks] out of the land of Egypt."*

Exodus 13:17-18, AMP

When God first brought the Israelites out of the Egypt, he led them through the wilderness. He did not want them to go near the Philistines. If they would have seen the possibility of war, they would have changed their minds and returned to Egypt. They were going to have to become warriors to take over the Promised Land, but God was going to show them a mighty victory over the Egyptians before forcing them into battle.

They would have returned to Egypt if they saw war. They constantly complained and murmured they should return to Egypt. They would have preferred to die in Egypt or the wilderness than to take over the Promised Land. Every time something went wrong in their minds, they complained they should have just stayed in Egypt.

They were bound by the grasshopper complex. This group of Israelites had been slaves all their lives. They had been beaten. They had been abused. They had been put into cruel bondage. Their spirits had been totally crushed by the slavery they were put through.

They didn't see themselves as warriors. They saw themselves as slaves. They saw themselves as grasshoppers. They saw themselves as insignificant. They saw themselves as weak. They saw themselves as worthless. They saw themselves as unable to obey God.

God called them a great nation. They didn't see themselves as a nation. They saw themselves as slaves. God had broken them out of their comfort zone. It was a horrible torturous life back in Egypt, but they wanted to go back into bondage because they were used to it. They felt comfortable there in bondage.

Change is scary. Doing something you've never done before is scary. Their mindsets were used to bondage. They knew what would happen there. They worked till their bodies were sick. They were beaten. They were yelled at. After years of this, their minds grew accustomed to it. They began to think it is how they should be treated. They began to think it is what they deserved. They were called slaves, and they believed they really were slaves.

The circus will bind a baby elephant to a post with a rope. The baby elephant will tug and tug, never to break free. It simply isn't strong enough to break the rope. By the time it is grown up, it will have already given up. In its mind it knows it can't break the rope. It has accepted its fate in life. It could break the rope with a simple tug, but it tried so many times before and failed. It has given up hope.

The majority of prisoners will end up in jail again. Only a few of them truly have their lives changed when they get out. They may be paroled from jail, but they're still in prison in their minds. Unless they give their hearts to God and begin renewing their minds by the Bible, the majority of them will end right back up in jail again.

A little girl is sexually abused. When she grows up, she will usually have one of two reactions. She may be very sexually promiscuous and give her body for sex to all kinds of men because she doesn't believe it has any more value than this. Or she may avoid sex and men altogether seeing sex as something dirty and evil. Both of these reactions come from a prison which has been built up in the mind of the little girl.

Poverty is a Prison

> *"(For the weapons of our warfare are not carnal, but mighty through God <u>to the pulling down of strong holds</u>;) Casting down imaginations, and every high thing that exalteth itself against the knowledge of God, and bringing into captivity every thought to the obedience of Christ;"*
> 2 Corinthians 10:4-5

You may have been raised poor. Your grandpa was poor, your daddy was poor, and you're poor. You went to a poor school and had poor friends. You may have been told you are just one of the poor people. That kind of talking and thinking will produce a stronghold in your mind. We'll call this castle, "We're just poor folk."

If you're going to go into the land of prosperity God has promised you, then you will have to destroy castle, "We're just poor folk." You can beg and plead to God all you want for Him to get rid of it, but He won't do your job for you. He told the Israelites to take the land. He tells you to take your land. You are going to have to pull down that stronghold, "We're just poor folk." God will help you, but He isn't going to do it for you.

You may have a different castle standing in your way. It may be castle, "I'm too stupid." Your teacher may have called you stupid in the 3rd grade and you accepted it. You started calling yourself stupid. Your parents decided you were a little stupid also. They might not have ever done it, but you saw them as introducing your family, "These are our children: John, Mary, and Stupid."

Someone else reading this may have been voted least likely to succeed in high school. So Satan came along and built the castle, "I'll never amount to much." So you never did anything better than just mediocre. Whenever you've thought about doing something bigger, the guards for castle, "I'll never amount to much," peak over the walls and mock you. So you've settled into a just-getting-by existence.

Your father may have called you lazy one day, and it became a stronghold. Castle, "You're lazy," was built in your mind. You would go to church today, but you're too lazy. You would study real estate and home improvement during some of your free time, but you're too lazy. If you ever start doing more than the minimum work required, the guards yell down from the gates, "Don't forget you're just lazy."

You get saved and go to church for the first time. Pastor "I'm too Educated for My Own Good" gets up and tells you how prosperity isn't for today. He tells you God has a reason why you're poor, sick, and confused. He tells you it's for God's Glory. He just made some to be rich, but you're one of the poor ones for suffering. Satan loves manmade theology so he gets to build big, beautiful castle, "You're suffering for God's Glory." He puts stain glass windows in that one so it looks like a church.

All of those ideas are strongholds built in your mind. I'm sure there are dozens more we could cover. Anything that exalts itself against what God has said and keeps you in bondage is a stronghold. It's a prison. It's your giant. If you want to enter your promised land of prosperity, you are going to have to destroy it and tear down those walls!

Confidence in God Produces Victory

"And as he talked with them, behold, there came up the champion, the Philistine of Gath, Goliath by name, out of the armies of the Philistines, and spake according to the same words: and David heard them. And all the men of Israel, when they saw the man, fled from him, and were sore afraid. And the men of Israel said, Have ye seen this man that is come up? surely to defy Israel is he come up: and it shall be, that the man who killeth him, the king will enrich him with great riches, and will give him his daughter, and make his father's house free in Israel. And David spake to the men that stood by him, saying, <u>What shall be done to the man that killeth this Philistine</u>, and taketh away the reproach from Israel? for <u>who is this uncircumcised Philistine, that he should defy the armies of the living God</u>? And the people answered him after this manner, saying, So shall it be done to the man that killeth him. And Eliab his eldest brother heard when he spake unto the men; and Eliab's anger was kindled against David, and he said, Why camest thou down hither? and with whom hast thou left those few sheep in the wilderness? <u>I know thy pride, and the naughtiness of thine heart</u>; for thou art come down that thou mightest see the battle."
1 Samuel 17:23-28

The Grasshopper Complex

David faced his giant. Goliath was a giant. He came out to the army of Israel and challenged them for 40 days straight. He wanted a one-on-one battle with the mightiest man in Israel. All the men of Israel fled from him when he came out. Not a one of these soldiers was willing to face Goliath. Not even Saul, who stood head and shoulders above every other man in Israel, was willing to face Goliath.

Young teenage David, the shepherd, comes bringing food. The first question out of his mouth was, "What do I get if I kill him?" They told him he would be given great riches, the king's daughter, and freedom from taxes. His brother got angry at David and accused him of pride. Fearful people will always accuse people with faith of pride. When you start believing God, you can guarantee some of your Christian brothers/sisters will accuse you of pride also.

David then asks a second group if he really gets a bunch of money, a woman, and no more taxes. They tell him the same thing. He will get cash and that motivates anybody. He's a teenage boy so a pretty woman really motivates him. And not having any taxes is the dream of everybody who receives great riches. So he immediately goes to Saul.

"And David said to Saul, Let no man's heart fail because of him; thy servant will go and fight with this Philistine."
1 Samuel 17:32

David tells Saul he will go defeat the Philistine. Saul accuses him of being just a boy. Then David tells him about the times God protected him from both a lion and bear. God delivered him before, and God will deliver him again.

"Thy servant slew both the lion and the bear: and this <u>uncircumcised Philistine</u> shall be as one of them, seeing he hath defied the armies of the living God. David said moreover, The <u>LORD that delivered me</u> out of the paw of the lion, and out of the paw of the bear, he will deliver

> *me out of the hand of this Philistine. And Saul said unto David, Go, and the LORD be with thee."*
> 1 Samuel 17:36-37

The key phrases from these verses are the "uncircumcised Philistine" and "The Lord that delivered me." He was confident in his ability to defeat the Philistine because of the covenant he had with God. Circumcision is the sign of the covenant. So he was telling Saul, "My covenant God will deliver this non-covenant man into my hand." That was the difference between David and Goliath. David had and knew his covenant with God. Goliath didn't have a covenant with God. David's confidence was based on his faith in God's covenant with Israel.

> *"Then said David to the Philistine, Thou comest to me with a sword, and with a spear, and with a shield: but I come to thee in the name of the LORD of hosts, the God of the armies of Israel, whom thou hast defied. This day will the LORD deliver thee into mine hand; and I will smite thee, and take thine head from thee; and I will give the carcases of the host of the Philistines this day unto the fowls of the air, and to the wild beasts of the earth; that all the earth may know that there is a God in Israel."*
> 1 Samuel 17:45-46

Did David walk out on the battlefield and tell God to kill Goliath? Did he stand there and pray for God to deal with the giant standing in front of him? No. Read all of I Samuel 17. David never prays at all in the whole chapter. He never even asks God if it is OK to go up and fight the Philistine. All he did was ask what he was going to get for killing the Philistine. He never questioned whether he could kill the Philistine. He knew he could do that simply because of his covenant. He just wanted to know if they were going to make it worth his time.

He simply announced his victory when he got to the battlefield. He said what he was going to do. He said the Lord was going to give him the ability to kill Goliath and take his head. And then he said he was going to kill all the host of the Philistines. He got up there and said just like a teenager, "I'm going to kill you Goliath and then I'm going to kill your whole army too."

There definitely wasn't any fear in David. People would say he had self-confidence, but that wouldn't be accurate. We need to come up with a new term to describe believers like David, "God-confidence." Sometimes we need to quit our praying and step out in faith in what God has already told us to do. Take a look at this often misquoted scripture...

> *"And <u>Moses said</u> unto the people, Fear ye not, <u>stand still, and see the salvation of the LORD</u>, which he will shew to you to day: for the Egyptians whom ye have seen to day, ye shall see them again no more for ever. The LORD shall fight for you, and ye shall hold your peace. And the <u>LORD said</u> unto Moses, <u>Wherefore criest thou unto me? speak unto the children of Israel, that they go forward:</u>"*
> Exodus 14:13-15

That sounds like a great spiritual statement, "Stand still, and see the salvation of the Lord." I've heard ministers preach great messages on why we should stand still and see the Lord's deliverance occur. It sounds oh so spiritual. That was what Moses said. What did God say? God said, "Why are you praying to me? Tell the people to go forward."

"Go forward" and "stand still" are two completely different things. Moses told the people to stand there and wait for God. God told them to quit standing there and move forward. Moses was waiting for God to do something. God was waiting for the children of Israel to do something. God did not part the Red Sea until they started moving toward it.

This happens a lot in the relationship between God and man. For example, Jesus told the church to go into all the world and preach the gospel. Somehow that message has been changed in the modern day church to sit on your butt in the church and pray for people to come in. We say wait. God says go. How different could those messages get?

David didn't "stand still" in the presence of Goliath. That would have been a good way to get his skull chopped in two. He went forward. He ran at Goliath. He met him head-on at full speed. He already knew the covenant and promises of God. He knew God's will in this situation. He didn't need to wait any longer and hold a board meeting to see if he should kill him. The purpose of prayer is to fellowship with God and find out His will. Once you know His will and His direction GO!

God-confidence is when you fully believe everything God has said about you. Spend time studying His Word. See what He says about you in His Word. He calls you things like the righteousness of God, a new creature, an overcomer, more than a conqueror, a king in life, and a son of God. People might have called you stupid, a failure, or a good-for-nothing. Let God be true, and every man a liar.

What people say is just their opinion. What God says is a fact. If people disagree with God, they're wrong. You're a mighty man/woman of God just like David and there are giants standing in front of your prosperity. Those giants are the wrong concepts you have about who God is, who you are, and who your real enemy is. God isn't going to kill those giants for you. He is going to empower you to take up your slingshot and kill them. GO!

It's Time for Heroes

> *"For you are still [unspiritual, having the nature] of the flesh [under the control of ordinary impulses]. For as long as [there are] envying and jealousy and wrangling and factions among you, are you not unspiritual and of the flesh, <u>behaving yourselves after a human standard</u> and <u>like mere (unchanged) men</u>?"*
> 1 Corinthians 3:3, AMP

Paul tells the Corinthians they are behaving like humans. They're acting like mere men. They aren't supposed to act this way. They have become new creatures, yet they're acting like normal unchanged people. It reminds me of Superman. In the movie and comics he was mild mannered Clark Kent during the day. He was klutzy and clumsy. He was shy and didn't act too sure of himself. When there was trouble, he'd change into his cape and he was Superman. He could leap tall buildings in a single bound and run faster than a locomotive.

You can't leap tall buildings, but God said you can move mountains. You're not a normal human anymore. You are a new creation. This world is no longer your home. Sin no longer has power over you. Demons no longer have power over you. Your past no longer has power over you. Poverty no longer has power over you.

David knew his covenant and was strong. Joshua and Caleb knew their covenant and were strong. The children of Israel didn't know their covenant. They were weak, slavery minded, and thought of themselves as grasshoppers. They saw themselves as zeros instead of heroes.

That might have been what you were thinking when I made the Superman comments above. You might not see yourself as a hero yet. All your life you might have been a big fat zero. When you got born again, God made you a hero. You're here to set someone free. You may never preach or teach. You may be called to lay hands on people. You may be called to say kind words to people to encourage them. You may be and probably are called to write checks which set people free from financial bondage.

Quit being a zero and start acting like the hero God already says you are. Your problem is you don't know who you are. You define yourself by your past. God defines you by your future. When the angel of God came to Gideon, he was hiding behind a winepress. The angel called him a mighty man of valor.

"And there came an angel of the LORD, and sat under an oak which was in Ophrah, that pertained unto Joash

*the Abi-ezrite: and his son Gideon threshed wheat by the winepress, <u>to hide it</u> from the Midianites. And the angel of the LORD appeared unto him, and said unto him, The LORD is with thee, <u>thou mighty man of valour</u>. And Gideon said unto him, Oh my Lord, if the LORD be with us, why then is all this befallen us? and where be all his miracles which our fathers told us of, saying, Did not the LORD bring us up from Egypt? but now the LORD hath forsaken us, and delivered us into the hands of the Midianites. And the LORD looked upon him, and said, **<u>Go</u>** in this thy might, and thou shalt save Israel from the hand of the Midianites: have not I sent thee? And he said unto him, Oh my Lord, wherewith shall I save Israel? behold, my family is poor in Manasseh, and I am the least in my father's house. And the LORD said unto him, Surely I will be with thee, and thou shalt smite the Midianites as one man."*
Judges 6:11-16

The angel told Gideon that the Lord was with him and he was a mighty man of valor. He didn't look much like a man of valor hiding behind the winepress. His past didn't look much like a mighty man of valor. His mouth didn't sound much like a mighty man of valor. He sounded a lot like Moses did. He made all kinds of excuses of why the Lord must not be with him. The Lord looked at him and said, "GO in this THY Might, and THOU shalt save Israel…"

Was Gideon going alone? No. God was going with Him. Here is the key. God wasn't going without him. They were going together. God supplies the power, the ability, and the wisdom. You're the one who does the Going. God has given you the power to get wealth, but you're the one who has to physically go out there and get it. He isn't going to go get it for you and bring it to you while you sit there.

If you continue to do the things you've always done, you'll continue to have what you've always had. You'll have to do something you've never done before to experience blessings you've never experienced before. God wants to answer your prayers for prosperity, but He will never change His ways of doing things. His plan is to transform your way of thinking until you think about things the same way He does.

You don't have confidence in God if you don't believe what He has said about you. If you still believe you're a lowly, poor worm barely making it through life, then you'll never experience much of His blessings. If your mind continues to be bound by the prison of the past, then you'll never be free to step into the future God has prepared for you.

> *"When I blow with a trumpet, I and all that are with me, then blow ye the trumpets also on every side of all the camp, and say, The sword of the LORD, <u>and of Gideon</u>."*
> Judges 7:18

They weren't going to shout just "the sword of the Lord." They were going to shout, "The sword of the Lord, and of Gideon." They were a team. Without God, Gideon could do nothing. Without Gideon, God would have done nothing. Repeat this several times, "Without God, I can do nothing. Without me, God will do nothing. We're a team and He's in charge."

Meditate in the Word to Set Your Mind Free

> *"This book of the law shall not depart out of thy mouth; but thou shalt meditate therein day and night, that thou mayest observe to do according to all that is written therein: for <u>then thou shalt make thy way prosperous</u>, and then thou shalt have good success."*

> *"This Book of the Law shall not depart out of your mouth, but you shall meditate on it day and night, that you may observe and do according to all that is written in it. For then <u>you shall make your way prosperous</u>, and <u>then you shall deal wisely</u> and have good success."*

Joshua 1:8, AMP

Let's say that I owned everything in the world and had multiple trillions in the bank. I came up to you one day and whispered to you that I could teach you the secret of prosperity. Would you want to listen to what I had to say? I thought you would. Well, God has the cattle on a thousand hills and everything on earth is His. He came up to Joshua one day and told him the secret of prosperity. It is recorded for us right here in Joshua 1:8.

He says that meditation in His Word will cause you to do all that was written in it. Doing the Word will make your way prosperous. You will deal wisely in all the affairs of life. You will have good success. Good success is when you have an abundance of money, your wife still loves you, and you have peace in your heart. Bad success is when you have money, but you're lonely and hopeless. God wants you to have good success.

Meditation alone wasn't the key to prosperity. Meditation would enable Joshua to do all that was written in the Book. The blessing was to obey God. This means that without meditation Joshua would not have the ability to obey God. Let that sink into your thinking for a while. This verse is for you also since it is written in the Word of God. If you don't spend time meditating in the Word of God, you will not be able to obey the Word of God.

Notice He didn't say reading the Word would cause us to obey it. Many believers simply read their allotted two or three chapters a day as quickly as possible. He didn't even say study it. He does tell us to study and to search the Word in other places. We are told here that the key to our prosperity is to meditate in the Word so we can do it.

Meditation is the Hebrew word "hagah." It means, "murmur, mutter, meditate, roar, imagine." It speaks of doing a mental exercise where you quietly speak while thinking on the scripture. You "see" the scripture in your mind. You see it taking place. Meditation is getting into the Word much deeper than simply reading over it quickly. When you're meditating, you're going to speak the Word while seeing it in application in your life.

Your mind thinks in pictures already. If I tell you to think about a dog, you don't sit there with the letters d-o-g in your mind. You actually picture a dog. The dog you see might be quite a bit different than the dog I'm thinking of. I can be more specific though, and your picture will get more specific. Think of an eighty pound golden retriever with big brown eyes, a long slobbery tongue hanging out, and floppy ears. The image you get in your mind is going to be a lot closer to what I am thinking now as long as you've seen a golden retriever before.

So meditation is simply us stopping and taking the time to read the scripture out loud, apply it to our own lives, and see it taking place. When God told Joshua to do this he only had the first five books of the Bible available to him. He was to meditate on the Law. He was to see and talk about Himself doing what the Law required. If he did this, he would be able to follow the Law. If he didn't he would find himself unable to follow the law.

As New Testament believers, we have an abundance of books and scriptures we can meditate on. You should start your meditation in the New Testament, especially in the epistles. These are letters to the churches. They are letters from God written to you. You will find many of them talk about what God has made you as a new creation, especially in Paul's letters. Paul had the greatest revelation of our redemption.

You should start meditating on seeing yourself the way God sees you. In the past, you have seen yourself as a failure. You have seen yourself poor. You have seen yourself as being a $6 an hour worker at McDonald's. God sees you as so much greater than that. You need to begin seeing yourself the way He sees you.

"And all of us, as with unveiled face, [because we] continued to behold [in the Word of God] <u>as in a mirror</u> the glory of the Lord, are constantly being transfigured

into His very own image in ever increasing splendor and from one degree of glory to another; [for this comes] from the Lord [Who is] the Spirit."
2 Cor 3:18, AMP

As we look into the Word of God, we see Jesus. We see our redemption by Him. We are seeing ourselves just like looking into a mirror. We are being constantly changed into His image. The more we get to know Him and what He has done for us, the more we will become like Him.

He prospered. He never failed. He was full of the wisdom of God. Demons had to flee from Him. He was 100% obedient to the voice of God. He was led by the Holy Spirit. He accomplished what He was called to do in this world. No man could take His life until He laid it down.

You may say, "But that was Jesus." Yes, that was Jesus. Now, since you have accepted Him, He has moved into your heart. He has given you His victory and His ability. The same Holy Spirit that led Him is in you now to lead you in life. He paid the price for you to be free in every area of your life including your finances. He was God, but He laid down His godly glory when He came to this earth (people can't even look in the face of God and live because of His glory).

Spend time meditating on the things Paul writes in His epistles. You can begin seeing a new image of yourself. You are going to see a new creation that walks in wisdom. You are going to see a new creation who overcomes sin. You are going to see yourself as victorious in life. Your past self-image won't define you anymore. You will receive a new image from God on the inside of you.

**You may currently see yourself as a failure.
The Word of God will reveal the champion you really are.**

Chapter Twelve
Our Strength Comes From Praise

"If any of you is deficient in wisdom, let him ask of the giving God [Who gives] to everyone liberally and ungrudgingly, without reproaching or faultfinding, and it will be given him. Only it must be in faith that he asks with no wavering (no hesitating, no doubting). For the one who wavers (hesitates, doubts) is like the billowing surge out at sea that is blown hither and thither and tossed by the wind. For truly, let not such a person imagine that he will receive anything [he asks for] from the Lord, [For being as he is] a man of two minds (hesitating, dubious, irresolute), [he is] unstable and unreliable and uncertain about everything [he thinks, feels, decides]."
James 1:5-8, AMP

Throughout this book we have been discussing that the key to prosperity is to walk in the wisdom of God. We are to pray for wisdom, and are to believe we receive the wisdom we prayed for. God grants us the wisdom we ask when we pray if we have unwavering faith. Many times we show our lack of faith in our prayers within a few minutes of getting up off our knees. Satan comes immediately to steal the Word. Someone asks us what we are going to do now. You'll be tempted to say, "I just don't know what I'm going to do if God doesn't come through."

Satan won in your life already if you say that. You are to believe you receive God's wisdom for your situation when you pray. If you waver, then you will not receive anything from God. In fact, James actually goes further than that. He says you shouldn't even imagine receiving anything from God if you waver. Don't even imagine it. You're not going to get anything from God with that kind of attitude. Cry all you want. Roll around on the floor and bawl up a storm. Give until the cows come home. If you waver in your faith, you will not receive anything from God.

Without faith, it is impossible to please God. You can't do it. It is impossible. No one has ever pleased God without faith. When you pray for wisdom, you have to believe you receive the wisdom you're praying for. From that moment on, it must be settled in your mind. You have received wisdom. You may not know in your head what you're going to do, but you have received the wisdom of God down in your heart. At that moment, you have to make a conscious decision to quit worrying. You have to decide right then you're going to obey God and walk in peace.

A lot of people may say, "But I just don't have faith like that." That's a lie of the devil. When you were born again, God birthed faith in your heart (Rom 12:3). You have faith. It's in you. You have the ability to please God. You don't fall into sin. You choose to sin. You don't fall into worry. You choose to worry. Most of us have spent a lot of time practicing worry until we're extremely good at it. If you continually practice something 24 hours a day 7 days a week, you'll get pretty good at it.

> *"Be <u>careful for nothing</u>; but in every thing by prayer and supplication <u>with thanksgiving</u> let your requests be made known unto God."*
> Philippians 4:6

You have to decide not to waver and not to worry. It is a decision you make to obey God. To worry is a sin. This verse tells us to not to worry about anything. God is telling us it is a choice. You choose to worry. You can choose not to worry. What are you to do instead of worrying? You are to pray about everything and then give thanksgiving.

So once you have prayed for wisdom, you should immediately begin to thank God for supplying you with wisdom. Thank Him for it. Praise Him for it. You'll be tempted to talk about how you don't know if you received wisdom or not when you prayed. Instead, spend time thanking God for answering your prayer. Thank Him for supplying the wisdom He promised.

Spend a few minutes thanking Him and praising Him for the abundance He has supplied you through Jesus. Throughout the day thank and praise God for the wisdom He supplied you with every time you're tempted to doubt or say anything of fear. If you're tempted to worry and fear 100 times that day, then you'll be giving a lot of thanks and praises.

> *"Out of the mouth of babes and sucklings hast thou ordained <u>strength</u> because of thine enemies, that thou mightest still the enemy and the avenger."*
> Psalms 8:2

> *"And said unto him, Hearest thou what these say? And Jesus saith unto them, Yea; have ye never read, Out of the mouth of babes and sucklings thou hast perfected <u>praise</u>?"*
> Matthew 21:16

Thanksgiving is one of the most powerful tools we have. When Jesus quoted Psalms 8:2 in the New Testament, he translated strength as praise. God has ordained strength in praise. Praise stills the enemy and the avenger. So when Satan is constantly trying to pull you into worry, the best solution is to begin thanking and praising God. Praise is where your strength comes from.

Is it any wonder why most Christians are so wimpy and wishy-washy? God has told us our strength is in praise, but most of us don't spend any time praising Him except on Sunday. And then many times we may be thinking about lunch or what someone else is wearing that day instead of concentrating our hearts on the Lord. God doesn't want to just visit you on Sunday and have you lock Him away the rest of the week. He wants to be a part of your daily life.

Praise & Worship Keep You Full of the Holy Spirit

> *"Redeeming the time, because the days are evil. Wherefore be ye not unwise, but understanding what the will of the Lord is. And be not drunk with wine, wherein is excess; but <u>be filled with the Spirit</u>; <u>Speaking to yourselves in psalms and hymns and spiritual songs</u>, singing and making melody in your heart to the Lord; <u>Giving thanks always for all things</u> unto God and the Father in the name of our Lord Jesus Christ;"*
> Ephesians 5:16-20

Redeem the time. Make the most of your time. Don't be foolish. Be wise (here we see wisdom coming in again). Understand what the will of the Lord is. So we're finding out what God's will is. Don't get drunk with wine, but be filled with the Holy Spirit. We can choose to continually be full of the Holy Spirit. It's a choice. How do we do it?

Speak to yourselves in psalms, hymns, and spiritual songs. Sing and make melody in your heart to the Lord. Give thanks always for all things. If we do those things, we will stay full of the Holy Spirit. How often are we supposed to give thanks? Always. You are to always be praising, worshipping, and thanking the Lord. It doesn't say just praise the Lord on Sundays. It says to continually be speaking, singing, making melody, and thanking Him for all things. You should be thanking Him for all the things He has done for you!

It is interesting how God compares being full of the Holy Spirit with being drunk. A person drinks to get free from their fears, worries, and inhibitions for a short time. Life is too hard for them, so they turn to the bottle. They get drunk and they no longer have to think about any of their problems. Drinking in reality only makes their problems worse, but they can't stand being burdened down with those problems anymore. They have to get drunk for a moment of freedom.

God is telling us that offering praise to God can have the same effect on us. We're believing Him for wisdom (or whatever else you may have prayed for), but our emotions are hammering us. Our emotions are trying to get us to quit. They are all over the place. Sometimes, your emotions seem full of faith. Other times your emotions are down in the dumps. You just want to give up and quit at times. Taking time out to praise God will cause you to get drunk on His love. Those problems will quit bugging you. Praise will put you on a natural high.

If you continually look at your problems and continually talk about them, they will keep getting bigger and bigger in your vision. You eventually won't be able to even think straight anymore. If you turn your face around and begin talking about God, He will get bigger in your vision. If you praise Him for what He has already done, your view of Him will get better. Whatever you pay the most attention to in your life will take over your life.

I like to compare this to two mountains off in the distance. If you start driving your car toward the mountain of problems, it will keep getting bigger and bigger in your view. Eventually the mountains will completely surround you as you drive right into the mountains. You turn around and see Mountain God way off in the distance. He looks so small. He is so far away from you. Your mountains of problems surround you though because you kept driving toward them.

If you want to get out of the mountain of problems, you'll have to turn your car around. You will have to start driving toward God and turn your view away from Problem Mountain. Start praising God for who He is. Start spending time in worship of Him. Your view of Him will get bigger and bigger. Problem Mountain may still be out there, and you can see it in the distance. It looks so much smaller now though since you chose to drive in the other direction.

If you spend all week looking at and talking about your problems, then giving God an hour on Sunday just won't do the job. You need to start spending time with God everyday in worship. That's right. You need to give Him time every day. Take out 15 minutes of your day and just praise and thank Him for all the blessings He has given you. Thank Him for becoming poor so you might be made rich. Tell Him how much you love Him for going to the cross in your place. You can sing songs to Him or you can simply tell Him about your love and gratitude for Him.

Then throughout the day praise God whenever problems come to your mind (Satan will learn to quit hassling you with problems soon enough). Whenever you're tempted to complain, give thanks instead. Whenever you're tempted to sit there and worry, start singing a praise song. Put a guard over your mouth. Whenever you're tempted to say anything negative, praise God for His Word instead.

The thought may come to your mind, "This prosperity stuff isn't working. I'll never get out of debt." If it does, forget that thought and say, "Thank You Jesus for becoming poor so I could be made rich. I thank you so much for helping me pay off all these debts."

You may get the thought, "I don't know what I'm ever going to do to get out of this mess." Instead of saying that, give God thanks for answering your prayers, "I thank you God for giving me all the wisdom I need today to handle anything that comes my way. I'm so lost without you Lord, so thank you for your wonderful blessings and wisdom."

If you are like most people, your mouth has most likely been full of complaints and problems. If you want to go all the way with God, you're going to have to change that. If you want to be a champion, you'll have to think like a champion. You'll have to talk like a champion. You'll have to act like a champion.

Give up the complaining habit. It has no place in the mouth of a champion. Replace it with thanksgiving. Change your focus. Your focus has to move from your problems to your God. What has God said about you in His Word? Praise Him for it. Praise Him for the finished work at Calvary. Praise Him for deliverance from sin. Praise Him for prosperity through Jesus. Praise Him for healing through the cross. Praise Him for what He has done for you!

Once you start giving up complaining, you're going to find some people will think you're weird. They're not going to have anything to talk about with you as complaining is all they know. I've been to places where I think everyone's goal is to talk about who has the worst problem. It almost seems like a competition. Brother John has arthritis, but sister Shirley has cancer and plans to die in 6 months. Bob talks about how they repossessed his car. Margaret says that's nothing as they may be taking her house from her soon.

Those are the people who will think you're weird! You won't participate in the complaining competition. All you do is praise and thank God for all the things He has done for you and is doing for you. They probably won't even want to be around you anymore. You make them uncomfortable. They may even tell you not to be such an extremist. If you ever get that comment, simply tell them, "I'm extremely blessed, extremely prosperous, and extremely full of joy."

Cultivate An Attitude of Gratitude

"By him therefore let us offer the sacrifice of praise to God continually, that is, the fruit of our lips giving thanks to his name."
Hebrews 13:15

Start living in an attitude of gratitude. Thank God continually for all His wonderful works. Thank Him for even simple things in your life. Thank Him for the house you live in. It may not be the one you eventually want, but it is shelter. Thank God for your spouse. They may annoy you in 174 different ways, but thank God for the one good thing about them (and if you look hard you'll find more than one good thing about them).

If you live in the US, you are blessed. As a nation, we are the biggest complaining cry babies in the world. If you have a small apartment, an old rusted out car, a few clothes, and food, then you are richer than a majority of the world's population right now. You have something to thank God for. Don't complain about what you don't have. Thank God for what you do have. Then thank Him for things you have prayed for. If you've prayed for your own home, then thank Him for giving it to you every morning. He said He would give you what you asked for, so believe He did. Begin thanking Him for your new home today even when you haven't seen it yet. That is faith.

If you live in another land where poverty is everywhere, then don't let that stop you. You may have nothing to your name at all. You may have this book as your only possession. Thank God for it! It's the key to getting everything else you desire. Begin praying for the basic necessities of life. Thank God for giving them to you even before you see them. Once you start getting those, then pray for other things such as an overflow to give to others, a home, and anything else you need and want. Always remember to thank God as soon as you finish praying. Continue thanking Him for it from this day forward even if you don't see your prayers answered for months or years. Prayer and praise will change your life.

Begin thanking God for even small blessings you receive. You may have quietly prayed for a close parking spot at the mall. You got a space right up front. Thank God for it. You go to the airport, and you receive an upgrade from coach to first class. Thank God for it. Someone buys you a cup of coffee. Thank God for it. You find a sale on the exact pair of jeans you were looking for. Thank God.

Doing this is important to changing your focus. Most people have spent their whole lives looking at things they don't have. They spend all day thinking about and talking about all the things they don't have. In America especially, we live in a marketing driven economy. You may receive 2,000 or more advertising messages a day telling you all the things you don't have and what you're missing out on. Even the toothpaste is

New and Improved. These companies hire high paid ad writers who spend their whole lives studying psychology and how to make you emotionally desire things you often don't even need.

Don't watch the news. Their job is not to present the unbiased news. Their job is to get ratings. The more they sensationalize the news and fill it with horror and danger, the more money they'll make. They'll tell you about the depression, the recession, and how terrorists are out to kill everyone. They'll tell you about how overpaid the athletes are and how the government wants to raise your taxes. Think about this for a moment. How many times have you seen the news feature stories on good things God has done for people? They ignore the good and focus on the negative, because that is what gives them the ratings.

A mouth full of complaining is praising Satan for his works.
A mouth full of thanksgiving is praising God for His works.

The whole world is pushing you toward the negative. You have to make a conscious decision to focus on God and good. You are not of this world, and you are not to be thinking like this world. Yes, there are problems in the world. Yes, you will have problems. We're not ignoring those. We're just changing our focus to God, instead of the world. By focusing on God, He will give us the wisdom we need to overcome the world.

You are the Holy Temple of God

"Know ye not that ye are the temple of God, and that the Spirit of God dwelleth in you?"
1 Corinthians 3:16

We already read that praise, worship, and thanksgiving cause us to stay full of the Holy Spirit. Here we see we are the temple of God. He no longer dwells in a building made with hands. He dwells in our hearts. He has taken up residence in us.

You have probably heard people say the church building is the house of God. That is not accurate at all. The church building is where the house of God comes together. It isn't holy because it is a church. It is holy because we're there. God lives in us, not in that building.

You come together with other believers to praise and worship the Lord in unison. You come there to worship Him as one voice. You should already be continually praising Him and thanking Him in your daily life. You should already be bowing on your knees at home and spend time worshipping Him every day. If you were already a worshipper at home, then you wouldn't have so much trouble getting into true public worship. You wouldn't be worrying about what the person sitting next to you is doing or what the pianist may be up to behind your back. If the whole body of Christ could come together in true worship with one voice together, this is what we would be seeing...

> *"It came even to pass, as the trumpeters and singers were as one, to make <u>one sound</u> to be heard in praising and thanking the LORD; and when they lifted up their voice with the trumpets and cymbals and instruments of musick, and praised the LORD, saying, For he is good; for his mercy endureth for ever: that then <u>the house was filled with a cloud, even the house of the LORD</u>; So that the priests could not stand to minister by reason of the cloud: for the glory of the LORD had filled the house of God."*
> 2 Chronicles 5:13-14

The glory of the Lord filled the house of God. His manifest presence was there. He is always with us as He promised never to leave us or forsake us. In this verse, we see His presence filled the temple. The priests could not even stand up in His presence because so much of His glory was there. He came in during their unified praise.

You're the temple. He desires to fill you up with His presence. Praise, worship, and thanksgiving will cause your own personal temple to be full of His presence. You will be full of His faith. You will be full of His Spirit. The fruit of the Spirit will be evident in your life. The nature of love will start pouring out of you. Your desires in life will change.

You will see God's blessings pouring into your life when you have given yourself as a worshipper. Praising God is like giving God permission to be God in your life. You exalt Him as your Lord and your God. You make Him more personal to you. As you do this, you will see the whole Bible become more real to you at the same time. As you draw closer to Him, He will draw closer to you (James 4:8).

Conviction in your heart will seem stronger. His blessings will come quicker. God isn't actually moving anywhere. You're simply moving yourself closer to Him. Those mountains of problems are fading in the distance as you get closer and closer to God. He is getting bigger in your vision and everything else is getting smaller.

Spend time praising, worshipping, and thanking Him everyday. Take 15 minutes or 30 minutes and give yourself to Him. Sing songs of praise. Tell Him you love Him. Thank Him for everything He has done for you through Jesus. Just spend some alone time with Him everyday. I suggested 15 or 30 minutes, but God will be pleased with whatever you begin to give Him. You may plan to spend 30 minutes, but you look at the clock and see you've been worshipping Him for 3 hours one day.

Don't be legalistic. You're developing fellowship with your Father. It is a relationship. It isn't the hours you put in which count. It is the heart and the sharing that take place during the time. You may start praising Him for 10 minutes a day at first. A month from now you may want to start getting up earlier to spend 30 minutes or an hour with Him everyday.

I'm sure you have noticed I used the terms praise, worship, and thanksgiving interchangeably throughout this chapter. I did this as I don't want you to look at your worship time religiously at all. You're not doing it because I'm telling you to do it. I'm being very careful to make sure not to tell you how to do it as well here. It is between you and God. This time with Him is simply to share the love and appreciation you have for Him and everything He has done for you.

The time you spend alone with Him is the beginning of your life of worship. Concentrate on eliminating complaining from your vocabulary entirely. Give God praise every time you think about complaining. Any time your mind tries to worry, thank God for answering your prayers instead. Live a life of appreciation. Give Him the honor, glory, and thanksgiving due to Him continually all day.

Chapter Thirteen
Practical Wisdom for Daily Living

"The beginning of Wisdom is: get Wisdom (skillful and godly Wisdom)! [For skillful and godly Wisdom is the principal thing.] And with all you have gotten, get understanding (discernment, comprehension, and interpretation)."
Prov 4:7, AMP

The beginning of wisdom is when you realize you need wisdom. You realize if you want a change in your life, you must change your ways. That is the whole basis of change. Until you realize and accept you are responsible for the condition of your life, there can't be any help for you. Don't play the blame game, and blame God, your parents, your pastor, and your friends for all your problems. A common statement is, "Well, you don't know what they did to me."

It doesn't matter what they did to you. There is freedom in Christ Jesus for anything they did to you. It is up to you to reach out and receive that freedom. It's not up to anybody else. No one else can choose to live for Jesus for you, and no one else will determine the quality of your life and relationship with God either. Choose this day who you will serve. You can either serve God or you can serve your lowered expectations of life.

Another common idea is to blame God and His Sovereignty. You claim your life is a mess, because this is what God has called you to walk through. That is a lie. God wants you blessed and He has provided you with all the tools and ability you need to accomplish your full mission here on earth. It is your choice how much of God's Word you believe.

You are doing what you're doing in God's kingdom, because God can't trust you with anything more. God has given you all the responsibility you can possibly handle in your current state. When you operate in more wisdom, then God can bless you with more responsibility and greater works. When you prove yourself faithful in one job, He will promote you to the next one. If you can't be faithful washing the windows, then He'll never promote you to the church board.

We limit God. He is not the one limiting us. He has been waiting for you to get your act in gear your whole life. We often say, "We're just waiting on God." If you were to ask God though, He would say that He is just waiting on you. He is waiting for you to believe His Word and begin the process of change. He is waiting for you to search out and learn His wisdom. He cannot give His kingdom to a fool.

Wisdom is the Key to Godly Wealth

Wisdom is the key to godly wealth. Godly wealth isn't based on where you were born, how smart you are, what your grades were in school, your education, the color of your skin, or anything else the world may tell you. It definitely isn't based on luck. Godly wealth comes from the wisdom of God in your life.

> *"That I may cause those that love me <u>to inherit substance</u>; and I will <u>fill their treasures</u>."*
> Proverbs 8:21

Wisdom will cause you to inherit substance. Wisdom will fill your treasures. Those who love wisdom will inherit wealth. Their treasuries will become full. If you have been living in poverty all your life and your bank accounts are empty, then you haven't been loving wisdom. You haven't been searching for wisdom as a hidden treasure.

> *"I love them that love me; and those that seek me early shall find me. Riches and honour are with me; yea, <u>durable riches</u> and righteousness."*
> Proverbs 8:17-18

Those that seek wisdom early will find it. This shows a lot of diligence. You're getting up early and searching for wisdom. You love wisdom and are spending your time searching for it. When you do this, you will find riches and honor. They are hiding with wisdom. In fact, you won't just find riches, you'll find durable riches.

Proverbs is constantly comparing the wealth of the wicked and the wealth that wisdom brings. People who gain their wealth the world's way, through thieving, conniving, and feeding on others will eventually lose it. The world's way of doing business is to get all you can, and can all you get. They're out to get all the money they can by any means necessary. The majority of them will do anything legal to get all the money they can from you. The rest will even resort to illegal methods to get your money. The god of their lives is money. Money is a great servant, but it's a horrible master. Anyone who makes money their god will soon see the dangers in it. They get the money, but spend the rest of their lives stressed out by all the other crooks trying to steal it from them.

> *"In the house of the righteous is much treasure: but in the revenues of the wicked is trouble."*
> Proverbs 15:6

> *"The blessing of the LORD, it maketh rich, and he addeth no sorrow with it."*
> Proverbs 10:22

> *"The LORD will not suffer the soul of the righteous to famish: but he casteth away the substance of the wicked."*
> Proverbs 10:3

God constantly compares wealth gotten by the world's way of doing things with wealth He blesses you with. God's blessing will make you rich, but He adds no sorrow with it. The world's way of wealth brings sorrow with it. The more money they get the more empty they feel inside and the higher their assets, the lower their spiritual life. Their wealth doesn't ever bring peace to them. It simply brings them additional troubles.

Fear of the Lord is the Beginning of Wisdom

> *"The fear of the LORD is the beginning of wisdom: and the knowledge of the holy is understanding."*
> Proverbs 9:10

The fear of the Lord is the beginning of wisdom. It is respect for Him and His ways. You bow down to Him in reverence as owner of everything. Let me give you another definition for wisdom. It's God's way of doing things. God wants you to have wisdom. He wants you to know Him and His way of doing things. He wants you to do things His way. Don't just do things the way your little mind tells you. Do things His way. If you do everything God's way, that would be wisdom.

Worship Him first. Give Him reverence. You may have thought the last chapter about worship didn't belong in a book about finances. It has everything to do with your finances. Money has a lot of power. It is the root of all kinds of evil. It is an idol for a majority of the world. They will do anything for the almighty dollar. Putting God in His proper place of worship will go a long way in defeating the power of money over you. You can only have one god. Is it God or money?

> *"But seek ye first the kingdom of God, and his righteousness; and all these things shall be added unto you."*
> Matthew 6:33

> *"But seek (aim at and strive after) first of all His kingdom and His righteousness (His way of doing and being right), and then all these things taken together will be given you besides."*

Matthew 6:33, AMP

Seek first the kingdom of God, and all the things the Gentiles are seeking after will be added to you. They are seeking after clothing, food, houses, cars, etc. God says all these things will be added to you if you are seeking His kingdom first. The Amplified translated righteousness in this verse as "His way of doing and being right." God is always right. He wants you to begin doing things His way, because He is right.

Put God first in your life. Spend time worshipping Him everyday. Sing songs of praise to Him. Tell Him you love Him. Give up complaining and replace it with thanksgiving. Having this type of reverence for God (where you put Him first) is the beginning of wisdom. If anything else is first in your life before God, then you're not seeking wisdom God's way.

If you love anyone more than God, then your priorities are out of order. If you love your parents, your wife, your husband, your kids, or your friends more than God, then your life is out of order. If you spend time with them before God, then your life is out of order. Spend time with God and then spend time with them. Even better, spend time with them seeking God.

If you love pleasure more than God, then your life is out of order. You may work a hard job 6 days a week. You want to sit down and relax on that seventh day. Your flesh wants to stay in bed and watch TV. God wants you to go to church and spend time seeking Him during the afternoon. Which one do you do? If you're wise, you'll put God first. If you're a fool, you'll follow the flesh.

Diligence is the Basis of All Success

"He becometh poor that dealeth with a slack hand: but the <u>hand of the diligent maketh rich</u>."
Proverbs 10:4

I love the book of Proverbs. It is full of practical wisdom for our daily success. If you truly desire to be financially blessed, I recommend reading a Proverb everyday. There are 31 Proverbs so if you read a chapter everyday you'll read the entire book in a month. Do this for a year and you'll have read God's thoughts about daily practical wisdom 12 times. Study it. Read it in different Bible versions each month. Take notes. Meditate on it and see yourself applying what you read to your daily life.

As you read through Proverbs, you'll notice certain topics come up time and time again relating to success. One of the most often mentioned ones is diligence. It is the basis of all success. If you're diligent, you will become rich. If you're lazy, you'll suffer poverty.

Diligence in the Hebrew is "charuwts" which means, "a trench, a threshing-sledge (sharp), and determination." This is actually a pretty complex word. We often think of diligence as hard work, but it is much more than this. Hard work is only a part of it. Diligence is having a sharp focus and sticking to it until it is completed.

Diligence is simply being focused on the prize. I could compare it to an Olympic athlete. The athlete focuses on the gold medal the whole time they're training. That is the prize. They train for hours every single day. They eat right. They drive past McDonald's instead of their car being magically pulled into the drive-thru. They are focused on the prize. There are days they want to quit. Their bodies hurt. They keep going. They see their friends playing outside, but they have to train. They stay focused on the prize. Their body is screaming in agony in the gym as they work out with weights. They stay focused on the prize. Diligence is the drive that keeps them focused and pushing toward the prize.

> *"Do you not know that in a race all the runners compete, but [only] one receives the prize? So run [your race] that you may lay hold [of the prize] and make it yours. Now <u>every athlete who goes into training conducts himself temperately and restricts himself in all things</u>. They do it*

to win a wreath that will soon wither, but we [do it to receive a crown of eternal blessedness] that cannot wither. Therefore I do not run uncertainly (without definite aim). I do not box like one beating the air and striking without an adversary. But [like a boxer] I buffet my body [handle it roughly, discipline it by hardships] and subdue it, for fear that after proclaiming to others the Gospel and things pertaining to it, I myself should become unfit [not stand the test, be unapproved and rejected as a counterfeit]."
1 Cor 9:24-27, AMP

Paul compares the whole Christian life to an athletic competition. He says they only have one winner, but we each can have our own crown. Just like an athlete, we have to conduct ourselves temperately and restrict ourselves in everything. An athlete can never allow their body to rule them and tell them to stay in bed when they should be training. They can't eat ice cream sundaes when their body tells them to. They have to restrict themselves in everything. Notice that Paul says we're not running without definite aim. We have a definite aim in our lives. We're not boxing without an adversary. Just like a boxer would beat his opponent into submission, we are beating our own bodies into submission. We're telling it how to act and what to do, whether it complains, screams, or throws a temper tantrum.

Diligence is keeping your eyes on the prize. When you have a prize in front of you, you can overcome obstacles to get there. An Olympic athlete overcomes all kinds of obstacles to succeed. They overcome physical pain. They overcome feeling tired. They overcome their mind telling them they can't. They overcome fear. They spend years overcoming hardships.

They overcome, because the prize is worth more to them than the pain.

Mediocre just isn't good enough for them. They have settled once and for all in their hearts they will be the best. They will pay any price. They will take any step. They will overcome all hardships. There is a drive in their hearts to be the best. It is screaming in them to win. You've never heard an Olympic gold medalist say, "It's not whether you win or lose. It's how you play the game." That would be heresy to them. It would run against the grain of their whole being. They want to win, and they'll do whatever it takes to win.

Some of them turn to illegal drug enhancers such as steroids and other drugs. That drive to win is so strong they'll do anything including destroy their bodies. They'll risk destroying their reputations in front of the whole world. That prize is worth so much to them that everything else pales in comparison. They are driven to succeed and win no matter what it costs. They want to be a champion. The gold medal means life to them.

What is Our Prize?

"Yea doubtless, and I count all things but loss for the excellence of the knowledge of Christ Jesus my Lord: for whom I have suffered the loss of all things, and do count them but dung, that I may win Christ, And be found in him, not having mine own righteousness, which is of the law, but that which is through the faith of Christ, the righteousness which is of God by faith: That <u>I may know him</u>, and the power of his resurrection, and the fellowship of his sufferings, being made conformable unto his death; If by any means I might attain unto the resurrection of the dead. Not as though I had already attained, either were already perfect: but I follow after, if that I may apprehend that for which also I am apprehended of Christ Jesus. Brethren, I count not myself to have apprehended: but this one thing I do, forgetting those things which are behind, and reaching forth unto those things which are before, I <u>press toward</u>

the mark for the prize of the high calling of God in Christ Jesus."
Philippians 3:8-14

The cry of Paul's heart was to know Christ. He lost all things including his title as a Pharisee, his position in the temple, his country, his people, and his self-righteousness. All he wanted was to know Christ. He didn't just want to know about Him. He wanted to know Him and to experience Him. Paul said he hadn't apprehended his goal yet. He was still driving, pushing, and reaching for the goal. He was pressing for the mark for the PRIZE.

Paul is seeking God with all his heart, mind, and being. He is pressing toward God. The prize he wants is GOD HIMSELF. He wants to know God. That is the prize. God is our prize. If we draw nigh to Him, He will draw nigh to us. What greater prize is there in the universe? We are seeking God to know Him and experience Him everyday of our lives.

"And to know the love of Christ, which passeth knowledge, that ye might be filled with all the fulness of God."
Ephesians 3:19

Paul was seeking to know the love of Christ. He didn't want to just know about the love of Christ. He wanted to know it until it became a part of every area of his heart. He wanted to be filled with all the fullness of God. He wanted a deeper fellowship with God everyday and everything in him was driving him toward that prize. He was willing to overcome anything to reach that gold medal of knowing God. He was often beaten, whipped, thrown in the ocean, and left for dead. He called those things "light afflictions" compared to the glory of the prize he was after.

Are your eyes on the prize? Is He your heart's desire? Would you be willing to give up everything for Him like Paul did? You'll never be diligent in your seeking of Him until those things get settled. You have to become like that Olympic athlete. God is your gold medal. You have to be willing to do anything, overcome any hurdle, beat down fear, and follow after Him no matter what.

Will you continue to seek Him when your life is overwhelmed with His blessings? We studied this when we studied the parable of the sower. Satan will try using manmade doctrines to stop your seeking of Him. Satan will try persecution and tribulation to stop you. His most powerful tactic is to use the blessings of God themselves to stop you. When you're financially blessed and can buy all the things you want, will they pull you from God's presence? Will that 60 inch big screen TV you can now buy pull you away from your Bible study? Will the 35 foot fishing boat you've always prayed for keep you from church on Sunday?

If you're focused on the prize, you'll overcome all these things (notice I spoke of tribulations and prosperity as both needing to be overcome). God is the prize and nothing can be allowed to stand in your way of seeking Him. That is diligence in seeking God. You'll put away other things and keep focused on Him.   If you seek Him diligently, He will make you rich (abundantly supplied).

Are You Diligent at your Job?

> *"Seest thou a man diligent in his business? <u>he shall stand before kings</u>; he shall not stand before mean men."*
> Proverbs 22:29

God says that a man diligent in his job will stand before kings. God will promote you when you're diligent on your job. You will not stay hidden. You may think nobody notices you at work. You may be at the bottom of the totem pole and everyone seems to take you for granted. Your boss may be out to get you. God is watching though. When a man's ways please the Lord, He will even make your enemies to be at peace with you (Proverbs 16:7).

It's a sad fact, but many times Christians have gotten the reputation as the worst people for companies to hire. They're lazy. They complain a lot. They're sick a lot. They quit without notice. They're not committed. Christians have gotten that kind of reputation to some bosses and in some companies, because they've seen so many flakes. Some even quit their jobs and live by faith (which means they sit on the couch watching re-runs and eating cheesy-poofs). Who would want to hire someone like that?

You can confess prosperity all you want, but if you're lazy at work...you'll stay broke. Nobody will ever notice you. You won't be promoted. You may even get laid off. If you prove yourself unfaithful in a simple job for the world, why would you ever expect God to hire you? You think he puts an ad out for lazy, good-for-nothing people to work for Him? When Jesus picked His disciples, they were all working. They were fishing. They were collecting taxes. They were doing something. They were hard workers! Are you?

"Servants, obey in all things your masters according to the flesh; not with eyeservice, as menpleasers; but in <u>singleness of heart</u>, fearing God: And whatsoever ye do, <u>do it heartily, as to the Lord</u>, and not unto men; Knowing that of the Lord ye shall receive the reward of the inheritance: for ye serve the Lord Christ."
Colossians 3:22-24

This scripture was written to slaves. You may complain that your job is slavery, but it's not. You choose to go to work each day. This passage was written for people who were actual slaves. They were told to obey their masters in all things. Let me translate that for you. Obey your boss in all things. If he tells you to bow down to an idol in the office and curse Jesus, you won't do that. You'll quit and go work somewhere else. Barring the boss telling you to sin (lying, fornication, killing, etc.), you are to do what you are told at work.

Whatever you do, do it heartily as unto the Lord. You are doing it for the Lord, not for man. Your boss may be a jerk. Many of them are. You don't work for them. You work for the Lord. Do your work from your heart. Put your whole heart into it. Do your best. If you're simply the janitor, then you make the office as clean as anything they've ever seen. Make it as clean as the Lord would like to see it. Pray for wisdom to do an even better job.

If you're a salesman, then sell. Sell all day. Study your products until you know them by heart. Study the competition's products. Study until you know what makes your product better for your customers. Take sales classes. Pay attention during training days. Practice different sales presentations. Follow-up on customers. Learn how to counter objections. Become the best salesperson they've ever seen. Do your job as unto the Lord.

I've seen many people who were called as ministers who can't even hold down a regular job while the Lord is training them. Your calling may be as an evangelist in the future. Well, the sales field may be your training ground. The same skills you use to counter objections to the sale today may be used to counter objections to the gospel in the future. God will never promote you unless you're giving it all you've got at your current job.

Your job may be in accounting. Well, count everything. Take advantage of every training opportunity or class your company may offer you. If someone else does a better job than you, find out what they're doing so you can learn from it. No matter what your job is, you do as unto the Lord. If you make burgers at McDonald's, then you slap together the best, fastest hamburgers they've ever seen. Show up on time. Have a clean appearance. Don't talk back to your boss. If they offer to teach you another area of the store, then jump at the chance and learn it.

Ask for feedback on your work and don't throw a fit when you get criticism. Do a better job. Become the best worker you can ever be. If they don't appreciate you, who cares? Your promotion comes from the Lord. Your boss can do everything in their power to hurt you or even demote you. God is greater. If you're doing the job God wants to see from you, then your boss will find themselves fighting with God.

If they refuse to promote you when God feels it is time, then God may move you to another company or may put you in business for yourself. He is your boss. You're working for him. He will see to it you are rewarded for the quality of work you do.

Be Diligent At Improving Yourself

"The hand of the diligent will rule, but the slothful will be put to forced labor."
Proverbs 12:24, AMP

Are you working at improving yourself? Are you better equipped in everything than you were 10 years ago? Are you better at your job? Are you a better husband or wife? Are you a better father or mother? Are you better at managing your finances? Or are you just as stupid today as you were 10 years ago?

A diligent person turns themselves into a ruler. A slothful person will be put into forced labor. Are you a self-starter or does someone else have to put you to work everyday? Do you read? Do you read the Bible to renew your own mind? Do you read other books to get better at what you do? When is the last time you read a book to make you better at your job? When is the last time you read a book to make you a better husband/wife? When is the last time you read a book to better train your dog?

If you don't have a high school degree, have you prayed about going to night school or getting your GED? Have you ever considered the possibility God may send you back to college? Have you been open to that desire in your heart to attend a real estate investment seminar?

You're going to have to move out of your "comfort zone" to receive the blessings God has for you. You'll probably have to do something scary you've never done before. You may have to go back to school. You might have to attend real estate seminars. You may have to go to a sales training class. You may have to spend days at the library and check out 12 books on computers. You may need to attend classes on investing..

That's why we covered the "Grasshopper Complex" before we got to this chapter. As opportunities come across your path, you will have the tendency to say, "I can't do that." You will make up excuses. You may even invite a few friends over and have a pity-party like the Israelites had. If you have a Joshua and Caleb heart, you'll say, "I'm well able to accomplish whatever God has for me."

Let me tell you a little secret about God. He will never give you a dream in life that you can accomplish without Him. If your dream isn't too big for you, then it really isn't from God. God always gives His dreams and visions for us in God-size. They are not man-sized. You won't fit into it on your own. You have to have His help to accomplish your dream. He doesn't plan Himself out of the picture! If you know how to accomplish it or to complete the dream right now, then you're not thinking in God-size.

If your goal in life isn't too big for you, then it really isn't from God.

It's going to take diligence every step along the way to get you there. You need diligence in seeking God. You need diligence in your current job. You'll need diligence in future jobs. You need diligence to start a business. You need diligence to work on and improve your business. You need diligence in improving yourself in everything you do. You'll have to give up some of your useless chatting during work. You'll have to cut out TV time. You may have to give up some hobbies.

Chapter Fourteen
More Practical Wisdom for Daily Living

"There is treasure to be desired and oil in the dwelling of the wise; but a foolish man spendeth it up."
Proverbs 21:20

"There are precious treasures and oil in the dwelling of the wise, but a self-confident and foolish man swallows it up and wastes it."
Proverbs 21:20, AMP

There are precious treasures in the wise man's house. The foolish man spent and wasted all of his treasures. Both of these men had treasures. They may have even earned the exact same amount of money. One saved their treasures. The other one swallowed up their treasures. They wasted all of their money.

Have you ever met a person that can't hold onto a dollar? It just burns a hole in their pocket until they spend it. If they get a bonus on the job, it is probably already spent in their minds before they even get the check home. That's how I used to be. I couldn't hold onto money. The moment I got it I had to spend it. Even before I got it I had to spend it on credit cards. I had no restraint. Whatever I wanted, I wanted it now.

That's the whole goal of advertising. Copywriters are taught that if they don't cause you to make the purchase now, they will never get the sale. They try to convince you how bad your life will be if you don't have their product. They manipulate you into making a buying decision quickly. There is a jewelry store near where I lived who had at least 5 different going out of business bankruptcy sales over a period of several years (there are "bankruptcy" specialists who come into stores and hold bankruptcy sales by marking all the prices way up so they can discount them back down to around regular price again).

All marketing and advertising focuses on your emotions. They talk about how you'll "feel" with this great new improved product. They are out to get you to make an emotional decision immediately. They don't want you to take time to think about it or discuss it. They scream, "Buy now," because they know you'll have somebody else yelling at you to buy 5 minutes later. There are all kinds of sales tactics people use to make you buy now. For example, have you ever went to a car lot and heard a salesman say, "If we can make you a good deal, would you buy today?" If they can get you to say yes to that, they know they are already on the road to closing a sale with you.

If you're going to become wealthy God's way, you're going to learn how to overcome these buying emotions. For me, I had to institute a 24 hour period to overcome them. I made a rule that we never bought anything without a 24 hour period to think about it first. We couldn't buy anything without it. That means you have a shopping list when you go to the store and you follow it. That means you don't buy a shirt because you just have to have it. That means you don't buy a car because the salesman made you an offer you couldn't refuse. We've relaxed the rule on small items now that we have money, but I still follow it very strictly on most purchases. My wife and I also spend time discussing the majority of things we purchase.

There are precious treasures in the house of the wise, but the foolish man spends it all. When God led us in wisdom and our income started increasing, we still didn't have anything left over for a while. We spent everything extra we were earning. Our income more than tripled, but we still didn't have any money. We were spending it all up. We thought the increase in money meant we could just spend more when we went shopping. That was very foolish.

Danger in Debt and Credit Cards

"Render to all men their dues. [Pay] taxes to whom taxes are due, revenue to whom revenue is due, respect to whom respect is due, and honor to whom honor is due. <u>Keep out of debt and owe no man anything,</u> except to love one another; for he who loves his neighbor [who practices loving others] has fulfilled the Law [relating to one's fellowmen, meeting all its requirements]."
Rom 13:7-8, AMP

This passage is sometimes used to "prove" a Christian should never borrow money. This isn't what it is saying. You have to keep it in context with the passage. We are to pay our taxes. We are to pay whatever bills we owe. We need to keep out of debt and pay all our debts. Our goal should always be to owe no man anything. The only debt we can never pay off is our "love debt." The love debt to others will never be paid off as we need to keep giving and giving just like Jesus did.

It is not a sin to borrow money. There are many places that God has told us we would be lenders, not borrowers. If borrowing was a sin, then lending would be a sin also since you would be causing someone else to sin. Throughout Proverbs we are told not to be a surety for strangers (co-sign a loan for someone else). What is wrong is our casual nature about debt over the past few decades. People think it is normal to owe money on your house, on your cars, on your furniture, on your vacation, and on credit cards. Watch TV and read ads in the newspaper, and you'll see a majority of them not tell you the real price of something. They tell you only 99 payments of $19.95.

"The rich ruleth over the poor, and the <u>borrower is servant</u> to the lender."
Proverbs 22:7

If you borrow money, you are a servant to the lender. That bank you're borrowing from is now your master. That doesn't sound like God has a very casual attitude about debt at all. You may be a servant of God, but you're also a servant of your mortgage company, your credit card company, and your car loan company. You're working all week long to make them wealthy. Is Jehovah your master or is it someone named VISA?

One of the reasons we got ourselves so far in debt in the first place was because of credit cards. They're one of the worst curses in today's economy. It is easy to spend money you don't have with a credit card. Just about every business takes credit cards. They're taught by the credit card companies that a customer using a credit card spends twice as much as they would if they didn't have a credit card. On average, a cash shopper spends only half as much as a credit card shopper. So of course stores cater to credit card users. They make more money off them.

We had a day where we cut up all our credit cards. We were in bondage to them. We settled that we just weren't going to borrow any more money. We couldn't control ourselves with them. So we weren't allowed to have them for several years. Eventually we got another credit card for convenience, but we have never spent anything on it we couldn't pay off immediately. If you don't have the money, don't spend it. Don't become your credit card's slave. If you can't control yourself, then you may need to cut up all your credit cards also. Get a debit card which takes money out of your bank account. Then you can only spend money you have (you'll still spend less if you go shopping with cash though).

What about major purchases such as cars and houses? The moment you buy a new car it depreciates. You may owe $25,000 on it, but it is only worth $17,500 when you drive it off the lot. That doesn't sound like a very good deal at all no matter what the car salesman tells you. The low mileage used car is a much better deal, but it is between you and God. Make sure you don't run right out and buy the brand new car just because you can afford the payments. Use wisdom in this area.

The same caution needs to be taken with a house. A home doesn't depreciate usually. It normally increases in value (although not 100% of the time). The problem with houses is the fact banks will try to convince you to buy the most house you can possibly afford. They'll try to get you on a 30 year loan at the maximum value your income will allow. What happens when both husband and wife work and one of you decides to start a new business or go part-time in the ministry? You now have less money available than you need for the house? You end up in a situation where it's hard to move forward in your life's purpose because of your second master, the mortgage company.

You would be much better off buying a house on a 15 year loan or one that is much smaller than you can afford. Pay it off in 7 years and then upgrade to the house you really want. You would have saved hundreds of thousands of dollars in interest and could probably get the home you really wanted paid off in another 7 years or so. For us, we bought our home at an auction. We had the house mostly fixed up and the loan paid off in 1 year from the date of purchase. If and when we buy another house, we will not borrow money on it at all.

There is Safety in Godly Counsel

"The way of a fool is right in his own eyes: but he that hearkeneth unto counsel is wise."
Proverbs 12:15

"Without counsel purposes are disappointed: but in the multitude of counsellers they are established."
Proverbs 15:22

"Every purpose is established by counsel: and with good advice make war."
Proverbs 20:18

God hasn't called you to be an island. He wants to put people in your life who can work with you and give you counsel. On your way to financial success, you may work with an accountant, a lawyer, a real estate agent, an investment broker, etc. They are in your life to keep you from doing foolish things. If you try to do everything on your own, you will make foolish mistakes that cost you money.

They are not in your life to get you to disobey God. For example, you know that the borrower is a servant to the lender. So you feel God's leading to begin paying off your house. Your accountant may tell you that you should keep this debt as a tax deduction. You need to ask him if he believes the Bible and specifically if he believes that the borrower is a servant to the lender. So while they are there to give you advice, don't let them give you ungodly advice. The lawyer shouldn't be telling you to sue people or to do anything dishonest just because it's legal to do so.

Begin looking for divine connections in your life. God may connect you with a person who does a wonderful job of fixing up houses for a living. You may team up with them to buy real estate. You may end up in a friendship with a bank worker who handles all the foreclosures. A member in your church may be starting a company and needs an investment partner. Someone you know may be the best cook you've ever seen and you end up creating a cookbook with them. Look for opportunities. They are all around you. The key is to be open to those divine connections and to listen to your heart.

"He that walketh with wise men shall be wise: but a companion of fools shall be destroyed."
Proverbs 13:20

Surround yourself with godly people who believe and obey the Bible. It may be difficult at first, but begin praying that God would give you these divine connections. You may even need to start your own church club, "God's Future Millionaires." Study the things you've learned in this book and pray over them together. You need good friends who can carry you and encourage you when the going gets tough. The average church member has not renewed their mind and Satan will often use them to try to discourage you or to tell you to stop being so radical. Pray for God to send you divine connections.

If you're starting or want to grow your business, feel free to contact my office. We do business coaching and can help you improve your current marketing, increase sales, and decrease expenses. We can even hold you accountable to systemizing your business for maximum profits while decreasing the time you spend in your business. We work with businesses all the way from new start-ups to multi-million dollar corporations. We also have Christian Mastermind groups to connect you with other business people who care about you and your business. Find out more through my web site at: http://www.mymarketingcoach.com

A companion of fools will be destroyed. If you constantly associate with fools, then you will be destroyed. If all your friends constantly complain, act negative, and live any old way they choose, then you have a major problem. You're running with fools. If you play with skunks, you'll come home foul smelling. You're going to need a new group of friends. You need friends who encourage you to seek God and believe God.

A Wise Man Saves and Invests

"A good man leaveth an inheritance to his children's children: and the wealth of the sinner is laid up for the just."
Proverbs 13:22

A good man is saving an inheritance for his grandchildren. He isn't just thinking about his children. He is working on leaving an inheritance to his grandchildren also. Over 95% of Americans are broke by the time they're elderly. They leave little or no inheritance to their kids. In many cases, the children are often called upon to support the parents financially when they get older. It shouldn't be this way. The Bible paints a picture of a person who still has wealth when they're old. They leave so much wealth that both their children and their grandchildren get a share.

The average family is only one or two paychecks from being homeless. A lot of the problem comes from debt and making spontaneous purchases. It also comes from the whole poverty mindset. They have been taught to borrow money for purchases instead of saving for purchases. I'm shocked by how many "Quick Cash" companies can be found around most cities. People go to them and take a loan out on their next paycheck. Most people don't even have a couple hundred dollars saved up for an emergency. Do you?

People used to save for things they wanted. Instead now, we just buy on credit. We pay two or three times as much for those things once we finish paying off the interest. Plus, we've established habits that will keep us in bondage for years to come. We need to become savers instead of spenders. You need to immediately start a savings plan.

A good rule of thumb is to start taking 10% of the money you make and put it in a savings account. Don't put it in your regular checking account. Put it in a savings account. This is to save for your future and to save for any larger purchases you may make. It may be a struggle to start saving like this at first. You have already learned you should discipline your flesh to be giving 10% or more. Now you need to save another 10%. So you now should start living on 80% of your income. You may have to learn how to be more frugal at first. You'll have to cut some of your unnecessary expenses.

There may be a set of furniture you've been thinking of buying for your living room. Instead of buying that furniture on credit, save your money to buy it. It felt so good the first time we were able to go buy a set of furniture with money in the bank. Buying a car without borrowing was even better, but each one was a step in the process for us. Focusing yourself on a prize and saving to get there is much more satisfying than buying it on borrowed money.

Debt can be very deceptive. Buying a house for most people is a good investment. You have to pay rent no matter where you live. When you buy a house and have payments at the same level as the rent you were paying, then you're better off. You are actually gaining a little equity and ownership in the house with each payment. So borrowing money for a house can be a wise decision. Here is where the deception comes in.

You move into your nice new house, but you only have furniture for half the house. Your flakey mind starts telling you you need to go buy a whole bunch of new furniture on credit. Don't fall for this. Pray for the furniture you need instead. You may even want to go to the furniture store so you can pick out exactly what type of furniture you want. Make a list and then pray over the list of furniture you need.

Believe you receive the furniture when you pray. God has answered your request. So from now on, anytime you think of the furniture, simply thank God that you have all the furniture you prayed for. Someone may give you the furniture. You may get a bonus at work for some of the furniture. God could give you an investment idea where the profits pay for the furniture. Leave the "how" up to God. You simply believe He has given you the furniture you've asked for.

Thank God for your new furniture. Don't bow your knee to the VISA god. If you're praying for the furniture, but the back of your mind is thinking of using VISA, then you're serving the wrong god. Remember, a borrower is servant to the lender. Are you God's servant or VISA's servant? Who supplies your needs…God or VISA?

Give to the Lord and the Poor

> *"He that hath pity upon the poor <u>lendeth unto the LORD</u>; and that which he hath given will he pay him again."*
> Proverbs 19:17

> *"He that giveth unto the poor shall not lack: but he that hideth his eyes shall have many a curse."*
> Proverbs 28:27

> *"Then shall they also answer him, saying, Lord, when saw we thee an hungred, or athirst, or a stranger, or naked, or sick, or in prison, and did not minister unto thee? Then shall he answer them, saying, Verily I say unto you, Inasmuch as ye did it not to one of the least of these, <u>ye did it not to me</u>."*
> Matthew 25:44-45

When you give to the poor, you are lending to the Lord. The Lord says He will be the one to repay you. You won't lose out in giving to the poor. It is part of your financial commission. It's not God's will for anyone to be poor, and it's part of your job to help them. If people are hungry and have nothing to eat, feed them. Part of the reason God wants you prosperous is so you can help others.

If you feed and clothe someone, you're doing it to Jesus. You're not only doing His ministry, but you're also ministering to Jesus Himself. If you're prosperous and you ignore the cries of the poor, then you're ignoring the cries of Jesus. I'd hate to be in the shoes of a wealthy Christian who doesn't give to the poor or only gives a measly 1% to the poor. If you don't feed the poor, then you're not feeding Jesus.

If you feed and take care of the poor, then God says He will repay you. Give to them out of love, but remember that God will always take care of those who take care of the poor. Everything God has is yours, and you'll never lose out by giving to the poor. That's His ministry. You're doing the Father's business by helping them.

Use wisdom in your giving. Help people get back on their feet. Help the widows and the fatherless especially (James 1:27). Help those who really need your help. Don't be naive though. There are some people who could be working and aren't, and there are some who waste all their money on things they don't need. You can still help them. For people who aren't working when they are able, give them a job to do. Have them sweep the floor or do the yard. Then give them what they need (II Thessalonians 3:10).

Your end goal in helping people is to get them back to productivity themselves. Give them a hand-up instead of just a hand-out. If someone is constantly having financial problems, give them a copy of this book. Offer to help them figure out a budget. Ask God how you can help them best. Be careful not to judge people. You don't know their situations or what may be causing their problems. You are there to be a friend to those in need and to help them, not to judge them.

The Virtuous Woman is an Example of Practical Wisdom

"Who can find a virtuous woman? for her price is far above rubies."
Proverbs 31:10

In Proverbs thirty-one is the virtuous woman. Her value is far above rubies. She is valuable to God and man. The heart of her husband trusts in her, because she does good for him all the days of her life. Her wisdom and hard work is part of the reason for her husband's success in this passage. Her children call her blessed, and her husband praises her. She is a model of excellence and of wisdom for everyone.

Solomon wrote the majority of Proverbs. He is someone who had a lot of experience with women. He had 700 wives and 300 concubines (I Kings 11:4). He talks about contentious women and how it is better to dwell on the corner of a housetop than in a large house with one. Throughout Proverbs he often compares Wisdom and Foolishness as women calling to us. In this final chapter of Proverbs, we see the perfect example of a wise, virtuous woman. Listen up men, you'll learn wisdom too.

You could study wisdom in this chapter for days, but we're just going to do a quick overview of a few of the financial points. This woman is the perfect example of wisdom, so let's take a look at just a few of her actions. As you look at her, you'll see a perfect example of diligence. This woman is diligent in everything. She is careful with money. She is saving.

She invests. She gives to the poor. She runs her own business. She is everything you have been learning.

> *"She is like the merchants' ships; she bringeth her food from afar."*
> Proverbs 31:14

She is wise in her buying. She is like a merchant's ships. She doesn't just buy any old thing because it's easy or close by. She searches for the things her family needs. She acts like a merchant and finds a good deal for her family even if she has to go a long way to find their food and supplies.

> *"She considereth a field, and buyeth it: with the fruit of her hands she planteth a vineyard."*
> Proverbs 31:16

She invests their money. She considers the deal and purchases a piece of real estate. Then she plants a vineyard on it. She upgrades the property to make it more valuable and useful for her family. She is a real estate investor. She considered and planned the investment. She had the confidence to step out and make the purchase.

> *"She perceiveth that her merchandise is good: her candle goeth not out by night."*
> Proverbs 31:18

She is a hard worker. We see her rising up while it is yet night in the beginning of the passage. Now we see that she doesn't quit just because it is dark out. She continues on with her work. Some people complain they're too tired to seek God when they got off from work. They complain they can't read a book. All they want to do is watch TV. Well, that's foolish. The wise person doesn't quit just because it's night time. She is diligent.

"She stretcheth out her hand to the poor; yea, she reacheth forth her hands to the needy."
Proverbs 31:20

She is a giver. She is feeding and taking care of the poor. Even after all the work she does for her family, she is still willing to reach out to the poor. Becoming wealthy God's way is never about hoarding or keeping it all for yourself. It's about abundance and sharing the overflow.

"Her husband is known in the gates, when he sitteth among the elders of the land."
Proverbs 31:23

She is working hard while her husband sits on his butt talking with some old people all day. Just kidding! Sitting among the elders of the land means he is one of the rulers. He is judging and making decisions for the land. Behind his success is this wise woman. She does him good all the days of her life and he has become a success. She is a wonderful helper and has helped him be promoted to a leader in the nation.

"She maketh fine linen, and selleth it; and delivereth girdles unto the merchant."
Proverbs 31:24

She is running her own part-time business. She is earning additional profits from this business of her own. She is making fine linen and selling it. It's much easier to become financially free when you're running your own business. Instead of making someone you work for rich, you can make yourself rich. You eat the fruits of your own labor when it's your business.

This chapter was written thousands of years ago. God gave us the image of a strong, confident, business oriented woman way before anyone in our generation thought it up. This was written during a time when women weren't thought of as being able to accomplish anything. Yet God told us about a woman who bought real estate and ran her own business. Her husband was successful because of her!

Religion may try to hold women down, but God lifts them up. This virtuous woman both loves and cares for her family while still having a career. Instead of going out to work a job, she creates her own opportunities. A lot of women have figured this out in the past few years, and the number of women who work at home is growing dramatically. It isn't anything new. It was a pattern God showed us thousands of years ago.

You need to be faithful to your job and diligent in your work. Everything you do should be done as unto the Lord. God can bless you with promotions, pay increases, and bonuses through your job. You definitely need to open your heart and mind to God leading you through different doors as well.

Wealthy people don't get there from just working at a job. There are high paid occupations such as doctors which can be decently prosperous through just a job, but the kind of money they earn is nothing compared to high income business people. Wealthy people earn their money through business or through investing. They set their own income with God's help. We'll cover more on this as we get into the next chapter.

Chapter Fifteen
Finding God's Road of Success for You

"But thou shalt remember the LORD thy God: for it is he that <u>giveth thee power to get wealth,</u> that he may establish his covenant which he sware unto thy fathers, as it is this day."
Deuteronomy 8:18

The Lord gives you power to get wealth. It doesn't say in this verse that He is handing you the wealth. It is not going to rain down from heaven on you. He doesn't keep our money in heaven. If He were to print money in US dollars, they would be counterfeit. He doesn't desire to hand you cash. His desire is to give you power to get wealth.

You pray and God gives you a financial miracle. Let's say you can't pay your electric bill. You pray for a miracle, believing you receive, and someone at church comes over and hands you a check for just enough to pay the bill. God worked a miracle for you. Your bill was paid just like you prayed for. God will do financial miracles for you. He will help you in time of need and give you what you ask Him for. A financial miracle is just not God's best for you.

God wants you to live in the blessing, not just praying for a miracle. He wants you to be blessed and to be a blessing to others. He wants you to be the person He uses to give financial miracles to others. He has given you the power to get wealth. You have the ability and the strength to go out there and get the wealth.

A measure of success can come through your current job. God can bless you there and promote you. You can receive a pay raise and bonuses. It can be one way God will bless you, but most jobs have a ceiling on them. They only pay you so much. The very nature of a business means that the boss can only pay you about one-third to one-fourth of the money your position earns them. The rest goes to other expenses, overhead, and profits. So your job can produce a blessing, but it is limited.

God is unlimited and He can take the limits off you as well. To get to God's eventual plan of wealth for you will require you to take a step outside your job at some point. You will be required to act like the virtuous woman and advance into other areas of income. We saw from our study of the virtuous woman in the last chapter that she took care of her family first. She also purchased real estate, planted a vineyard, and created items to sell to customers.

In God's plan of blessing for you, He may have you work your job. You need to stay faithful there and prove to God you can be trusted as a worker and a giver. Then you will start finding other forms of income. You may start getting the urge to pick up books on real estate investment at the bookstore. You may be driving down the road and you constantly talk and think about how nice it would be to own and rent out houses.

You're doing your job. You're believing God for financial increase and blessing. You've been spending time worshipping and praying daily. You pick up a couple of real estate books at the library, because they just seem to stand out to you. You go to a real estate seminar or attend your local real estate investment club. You begin learning all you can about properties.

Then you begin taking action and start looking for houses. It could be low priced houses, ugly houses that need repairs, auction houses, houses in foreclosure, etc. You thank God for wisdom and get to work looking. After several weeks you find your first great deal on a house needing repairs and take it. You find a private lender to loan money on the house, and you buy it. Then you pray for wisdom to find a good contractor to begin repairs. The repairs go well and three months later you sell it for a nice twenty thousand dollar profit.

That is an example of the power to get wealth in action. You pray. You stay faithful to your work and to God. You believe and confess the Word over your life (avoiding complaining). God then begins leading you in a way to get wealth. The wealth doesn't just fall on you. Opportunities come disguised as work. It was a lot of work to find a house, fix it up, and sell it. God blessed you throughout the process, but you worked hard to realize that profit.

> *"So also faith, if it does not have works (deeds and actions of obedience to back it up), by itself <u>is destitute of power</u> (inoperative, dead)."*
> James 2:17, AMP

God has given you power to get wealth. You say you believe that statement from God. If you don't have works (deeds and acts of obedience to back it up), then it is without power. Believing means you take action based on your faith. To get to God's wealthy place will require many acts of faith. You're going to have to move out of your comfort zone.

It takes faith in God to step out into your own business. It takes faith to risk money you've worked hard at saving. It takes faith to believe you can do it. You may be bound by the Grasshopper Complex. Strongholds of fear and poverty thinking will try to hold you back. Fear tries to keep you bound and in your little comfort zone at work. You have to believe God and step out by faith into a larger world where God can give you greater blessings.

God Had to Change My Mindset

Back in the days of my poverty and horrible debt, I was simply praying for God to come along and give me a large financial miracle. I wanted out of the mess I was in. I gave. I prayed. I worked. I waited for God's blessings. Then I prayed for God to give me wisdom. Things began to change immediately. He didn't just come riding in on a white horse and hand me money. He first started changing me.

The direction I went was in starting my own home based business on the Internet. I had to learn computers so I sat there learning the basics of how to use a computer from books. I played around with the Internet and had to learn to use it. Then I spent quite a large sum of money on copywriting books and courses to learn how to write effective ad copy.

I purchased audio tapes and videos from other companies and launched off in my business to start selling those online. I learned how to design web sites and placed them online. I learned Internet marketing and started placing ads all over the Internet. Profits started coming in slowly at first. I was running my own business, and it required a complete change in my mindset. I wasn't just sitting around waiting for God to do something. I was doing something with His blessing.

Eventually I started creating my own ebooks (digital books), audio tapes, and videos which taught others how to design web sites and advertise online. I started teaching others how to do what I had been doing. I flew to seminars all over the country and was being paid very nice fees for Internet consulting with businesses. I had money. I talked about my mistake earlier on in this book. As I became more and more prosperous, I allowed myself to walk away from God. I stopped praying. I stopped reading the Bible. I eventually stopped going to church for a while.

Being poor and not being able to buy anything changed over to having money and being able to buy whatever I wanted. I ignored God. I just kept making money. Being poor is no fun. Being rich and not having God isn't fun either. The excitement of having money began to wear off on me.

Dissatisfaction with my life set in. I wasn't happy anymore making money and ignoring God. I cut the time I spent working and started seeking God again. I wasn't happy working in that business anymore so it has been sold to another company. You can still find some of the products I created during that business being sold all over the Internet by another company (Note: my current coaching business can be found at:

http://www.mymarketingcoach.com and my Christian business blog is at http://www.terrydean.org).

The mistake I made was being consumed with money. I followed God's leading when I started and it made me much more prosperous than I had ever been before. I allowed that to pull me away from my Bible study and prayer and then started becoming a person I simply didn't like anymore. That's the road hazard to watch out for. Don't allow God's blessings to pull you away from seeking His face. You'll become someone you no longer like. God has to stay God of your business, or you have no business.

Don't allow God's financial blessings to pull you away from your calling in the body of Christ either. You may be called to minister to people through your business. You could share Jesus with some of your customers or with your suppliers. I'm not telling you to witness to everyone you meet, but there comes a time where someone asks you why you're so full or joy…or you feel your conscience pricking you to witness to someone. You may be called to minister in other ways besides your business as well. You may be called to lead worship. You may be called to exhort people in the body. You may be called to teach the children in Sunday school. Don't allow money to deceive you and pull you out of your call because of God's blessings. Reread the chapter on "What About the Hundredfold Return."

You'll know when you have missed it by the lack of peace in your heart. If all you feel is dissatisfaction in your heart, then you've missed it somewhere. If there is no joy, then you need to seek God until you find out why. You may have taken a detour on God's plan or you may have allowed your motives to move away from His love. Your heart is your guide. Your heart is your compass telling you which direction to go. If God's peace isn't there, then find out why.

Allow the Holy Spirit To Lead You

"And they shall not teach every man his neighbour, and every man his brother, saying, Know the Lord: for <u>all shall know me</u>, from the least to the greatest."
Hebrews 8:11

"For as many as are <u>led by the Spirit of God</u>, they are the sons of God."
Romans 8:14

I wish I could give you a formula. Just do A, B, and C. Money pops out. That is what the "Give to Get" message has become to many in the church world. We're told to just give our money and expect God to multiply it back hundredfold. Put your money in the ATM machine and wait for it to come shooting back out multiplied.

That's not how God operates. You are a New Covenant believer. You have a personal relationship with God. The Holy Spirit has been sent to lead and guide you into all truth. God is a personal God to you. No one else can tell you what He has called you to do in life or where He is going to lead you. Sometimes your parents might try to lead you. They'll tell you to go to college and get a good job. That may or may not be God's plan for you. Someone may give you a personality test or "calling" test and tell you it has said you should do this-or-that. Those may be useful, but they have limited value. They put God and His callings in a box. Don't rely on any type of test to tell you what you're called to do.

You're not supposed to be led by people, by tests, or by prophets. Your pastor may have some insight into what God has called you to do, but he isn't your guide either. You are to be led by the Spirit. Old Testament people had to follow prophets because God didn't have a personal relationship with everyone. If you wanted a word from God, you had to seek out a prophet of God. Now God speaks to your heart. Look at this scripture:

> *"Delight thyself also in the LORD; and he shall give thee the desires of thine heart."*
> Psalms 37:4

    There are several ways you can look at this scripture. The first is that if you delight yourself in the Lord, God will answer your prayers and give you what you've been desiring. I believe that with all my heart. But also look at something else it could be saying to us. If you delight yourself in the Lord, he will give you the desires of your heart. He will put those desires in you. If you're focused on Him first and have put Him first in your life, then the desires in your heart also come from Him. If it your heart's desire to go to college to become a doctor, then that desire has been placed there by God. If your heart's desire is to own real estate, then you know where you should be focusing your attention.

    If your heart's desire is to start a business, then He is the one who put that desire in you. Starting a business can be a risky venture, so a lot of people go through life living way below their purpose because of fear. You'll have to step out of your comfort zone. You'll have to spend time learning all the aspects of business. You'll have to put money at risk to study, research, and find people who can work with you. It is not always easy.

    There are millions of Christians who go through their whole life working a mediocre job knowing there is something greater for them. They get up and go to work day after day...while their heart cries out for something more. You can have so much more. You can complete your calling. If you haven't already started, then use this book as your kick in the seat of your pants to get you moving. Make a decision today you won't just do what is most comfortable. You're going to step up to your next level in life.

    It is time for God's champions to come forth. It is time for people who love God to start taking action in the business world. For too long the church has looked at pastors and evangelists as being the only ones with a special calling from God. This is wrong! People who are "in the ministry" are simply those who are called to teach others in the church. Most real ministry takes place outside of the four church walls. You are called of God as one of his ministers.

A Christian business person is a calling. It is a ministry. You may be the only Jesus people around you ever see. We are called to be the light of the world, and we shouldn't be hiding our lights in the church building. Be someone who really cares about your customers. Be someone who has integrity in business. Be someone that other people can look up to and look forward to doing business with.

Christian business people who let their lights shine in the marketplace are God's champions. My prayer is that this book will raise up one million new champions for God. Be a champion. Step out into the marketplace and become what you've been created to be. You have talents and skills God has put in you, and you need to be using them. There is a business out there waiting for you that only you can do. Don't live life in fear...but step out of the boat like Peter and be one of God's champions.

Continually put God first in your life and obey His Word. Seek God and let Him guide you. He may give you new ideas in the company you work for which greatly increase their profits. You may get profit sharing on those ideas. You may have a desire to start your own Internet business like I did. You may want to start a baking company. You may want to start a cleaning business. You may want to buy land or houses. You may study books on stock investing. You may learn about commodity investing. You may go back to college.

So I can't give you specific guidance about what exactly you should do. That's not the purpose of this book. This book has been written to simply teach you His ways. So believe God has prospered you and given you power to get wealth. Give as He leads you. Spend time thanking Him everyday and avoid complaining. Confess the Word. Start using wisdom in your daily finances. Spend time with Him everyday and start examining the desires He has put in your heart.

I can't tell you His plans for you, but I can tell you a few principles about His plans. His plan will always be too big for you. They don't just come Super-sized. They come in God-size. He will never give you a plan you can do without Him. You'll need faith to complete His plan. You'll have to combat the Grasshopper mentality telling you why you can't do it.

You'll have to overcome fear as it is often the biggest roadblock to reaching your purpose. There will almost always be a training period where you learn through classes, seminars, books, mentors, etc. You'll have to learn and grow to complete the blessing He has for you. His plan for you is abundance for your life and to bless those around you.

The plan from God will require diligence. You'll have to keep your eyes on the prize (financial abundance) and work hard to get there. You'll have to stay focused during distractions. You'll have to make sacrifices and lay aside weights on the way to your dream. You'll have to be like the Olympic athlete who stays focused on the goal of prosperity for you.

Don't Be a Sucker for "Get Rich Quick"

"He that hasteth to be rich hath an evil eye, and considereth not that poverty shall come upon him."
Proverbs 28:22

I'm sure you've seen the ads or been to one of the meetings. Marketers promise almost instant wealth with little or no work. You see them on infomercials and they invite you to come to team meetings. They may be selling something different, but the pitch is always the same. It only takes a few minutes a day and you'll be on your way to wealth. There are network marketing scams, real estate scams, home business scams, auction scams, etc. Give them your money and they'll teach you the insider secrets.

The only place success comes before work is in the dictionary. If you're going to succeed at anything, you're going to put a lot of time and work into it. You may see a no-down-payment real estate course on TV. The information you learn from the course may actually be good. It isn't going to make you successful though without a lot more study and hard work put into it. You'll be reading more study material from other sources and also spending a lot of time to do the work.

A network marketer may come and tell you that all you have to do is talk to 3 people...and you could earn $10,000 a month. Fat chance! I know some very successful network marketers and they worked their butt off to succeed (including 12+ hour days often). They get vacations when they want and have money, but they worked hard to get there. The same goes for real estate, auctions, investing, home business, etc.

If you want success, you will work for it. You will put diligence into practice. Anyone who tells you different is out to sell you something. So are all these opportunities bad? No...not at all. You can often learn from them. Just don't think instant success will ever come without hard work. Let's take real estate. Real estate is a great way to earn money and to invest. Just because people make some exaggerated promises about it doesn't mean you shouldn't do real estate. You just need to know and understand the truth. Diligence is the key to success in God and in life.

The only reason why I'm discussing the "Get Rich Quick" philosophy is because Christians are often prime targets for it. You believe God wants to prosper and bless you. They provide a way to earn additional income along with proof (because with hard work those plans can often succeed). So many Christians jump on the bandwagon of broken dreams. They try something out for a month and then quit in disgust. They lost money and they lost faith in God because they assumed He would bless them.

> *"He that hasteth to be rich hath an evil eye, and considereth not that poverty shall come upon him."*
> Proverbs 28:22

If you slam yourself up against that scripture, then poverty will come upon you. If you expect to get rich quick, then you will lose money. God does not break His Word just because you thought He should for you. The wise man is diligent and prospers. The foolish man is lazy and poor.

Opportunity comes disguised as hard work. It will take you out of your comfort zone. You might not succeed on your first try. You'll have to study. It may take practice to experience success. You'll be put through a learning experience for a while. Faith doesn't give up. It keeps believing and it keeps going. It overcomes.

Are You Satisfied with a Mediocre Life or Are You Ready to Become the Champion You've Been Created to Be?

Chapter Sixteen
How to Become Financially Free from Debt and Poverty

> *"The Spirit of the Lord is upon me, because he hath anointed me to preach the gospel to the poor; he hath sent me to heal the brokenhearted, to preach deliverance to the captives, and recovering of sight to the blind, to set at liberty them that are bruised, To preach the <u>acceptable year of the Lord</u>."*
> Luke 4:18-19

Don't try jumping over the rest of the book and just reading this chapter. If you do that, you'll have no idea what we're talking about here as each chapter is building upon the one before it. You can't have a nice house without first laying a strong foundation. You've been building a foundation and starting work on the house all throughout this book. Now we're to the point many people bought this book to learn. God wants you out of debt and financially free. That is His will for every one of us.

It is never God's will for His children to go hungry or lack. He wants you to eat the good of the land. His desire for you is for you to be blessed and to be a blessing. He wants you rich (abundantly supplied). He wants you to have enough to accomplish your purpose here on earth, and to give to the poor and to ministries as He leads you.

The scripture above is the one Jesus was reading from the book of Isaiah when He was in His hometown. This was the message He preached everywhere He went. This was His message. He told people He was anointed. If they believed the message of the anointing, then they received deliverance from Satan's bondage. If they rejected the message like Nazareth did, they received nothing.

"That word, I say, ye know, which was <u>published throughout all Judaea,</u> and began from Galilee, after the baptism which John preached; How <u>God anointed Jesus of Nazareth with the Holy Ghost and with power:</u> who went about doing good, and <u>healing all that were oppressed</u> of the devil; for God was with him."
Acts 10:37-38

Poverty is an oppression of the devil. Jesus was sent to heal it. His message in Luke 4:19 was that He was sent preaching the acceptable year of the Lord. Does this mean it is just a year the Lord likes? No. The acceptable year of the Lord was a very specific year to the Jews. It was the Year of Jubilee. It was the year when all the slaves were set free and all the land went back to rightful family owners. You can read all about it in Leviticus 25.

"And ye shall hallow the fiftieth year, and <u>proclaim liberty throughout all the land</u> unto all the inhabitants thereof: it shall be a jubile unto you; and ye shall return every man unto his possession, and ye shall return every man unto his family."
Leviticus 25:10

Jesus was sent to proclaim liberty throughout the land. Everything that Satan has stolen from us must be returned. It is the day of our liberty. We deserved to be in bondage. We sold ourselves to the devil by sin. Jesus was proclaiming liberty to all the captives. He was proclaiming freedom from the curse of the law. He came to deliver us of every bondage Satan has put us in. This includes poverty. This includes debt. Jesus is proclaiming we're free.

It doesn't matter how far in debt you are. You may owe $100,000 or you may owe $10,000,000. Jesus has proclaimed it is the Year of Jubilee. Your debts are released. You are free. You are to receive your rightful inheritance back. You are a child of God and everything God has is available to you. It's time for you to begin receiving your inheritance.

Debt and Poverty Are a Curse

Poverty is not a blessing. It is a curse. It is a destroyer. It keeps you from fulfilling your God given call on this earth. Poverty will bind you up and keep you from being able to give freely and unselfishly into all the things the Lord is doing. If you can just barely meet your own needs, then you're very limited in being able to help other people with their needs.

Debt is bondage. Debt is not a blessing. Too often we have that confused. Borrowing money is not a blessing. Having to borrow money is part of the curse. Debt is part of the curse of the Law. Jesus defeated the curse of the Law for us on the cross and you are free in the Year of Jubilee.

"Christ <u>hath redeemed us from the curse</u> of the law, being made a curse for us: for it is written, Cursed is every one that hangeth on a tree:"
Galatians 3:13

You have been redeemed from the curse. Debt should not to be part of your life anymore. God doesn't desire His children to suffer the curse. You shouldn't be in debt and your church shouldn't be in debt. Debt is the world's way of doing things and buying things. It is not God's way. God's way is for you to live in the blessing and believe Him for your needs and desires.

One of the first places you should focus your financial faith is on being delivered from debt. Pray the Lord give you the wisdom and power to get out of debt. Lay your credit cards on the altar. Lay your vehicle loans on the altar. Lay your mortgage on the altar. Begin believing God for deliverance from the bondage of debt. God desires to pour His wisdom into you and to deliver you.

It is your Year of Jubilee. It is time for you to be financially free. All that money you're constantly spending to pay interest could be much better used in the preaching of the Gospel and growing in investments for you. If you don't believe God for freedom now, you'll spend half your life working to make other people rich. You'll pay interest to banks when the same money could be used to get thousands of people saved by giving.

Will you be a champion for God or will you settle for mediocrity? Will you settle for a beaten down daily existence of just barely getting by? Are you going to be like the Israelites who died in the wilderness grumbling and complaining without ever going into the Promised Land of prosperity? Or will you change your mindset and actions so you can be like Joshua and Caleb...and possess the promises God has given you?

Without Faith, It is Impossible to Please God

> *"But <u>without faith it is impossible to please him</u>: for he that cometh to God must believe that he is, and that he is a rewarder of them that diligently seek him."*
> Hebrews 11:6

It is impossible to please God without faith. It is impossible to receive God's promises without faith. You don't receive anything from God by works. You receive by grace through faith. God loves you. He has sent Jesus to the cross to take your place in poverty. Jesus became poor so that you are made rich through Him. You are abundantly supplied. You didn't deserve it and you could never earn it. It is His free gift to you.

You have to receive it by faith. All of the promises of God come by faith. It is not based on how much you give or anything you have done. It is based on the sacrifice Jesus has accomplished for you. He did the work. Now you simply have to receive it and walk in it. It is yours. Salvation has been made available to everyone since the day Jesus rose again from the dead. Anyone could receive it. You could have received salvation long before you did. It was a free gift by faith. You simply had to reach out and take it by faith. You had to confess with your mouth and believe in your heart that Jesus is your Lord.

> *"That if thou shalt confess with thy mouth the Lord Jesus, and shalt believe in thine heart that God hath raised him from the dead, thou shalt be saved. For with the heart man believeth unto righteousness; and with the mouth confession is made unto salvation."*
> Romans 10:9-10

Your deliverance from poverty is received the same way. You have to hear the Word. That's what you've been doing in this book. You have learned Jesus became poor so you could be wealthy. You've learned that God's will for you is financial abundance. Now you need to begin confessing it with your mouth and believing that message in your heart just like salvation. There are probably still areas in you where there is a stronghold. You might have been told you were meant to be poor. You might have been told how stupid you were. Whatever you've been told, there is a way to break down these walls.

> *"This book of the law shall not depart out of thy mouth; but thou shalt <u>meditate therein day and night</u>, that thou mayest observe to do according to all that is written therein: for then thou shalt make thy way prosperous, and then thou shalt have good success."*
> Joshua 1:8

> *"Casting down imaginations, and every high thing that exalteth itself against the knowledge of God, and bringing into captivity every thought to the obedience of Christ;"*
> 2 Corinthians 10:5

You need to meditate in the Word. Confess the Word about prosperity and see it taking place in your life. Take the prosperity scriptures of the Bible and confess them over and over again about your life. While you're saying them, think on them. See yourself in possession of them. Use the power of your God-given imagination to see yourself wealthy and prosperous. See yourself as a big financial giver. See yourself saving and investing for your grandchildren.

This is how you build your capacity for faith. This is how you tear down those strongholds in your mind. Use the Word of God as a sword and tear down every thought that is fighting against the prosperity God desires for you. To help you with this, a multitude of prosperity based verses have been provided for you in the last chapter of this book. You have to change your mindset before you'll see the change in your life.

Faith Without Corresponding Action is Dead

> *"Are you willing to be shown [proof], you foolish (unproductive, spiritually deficient) fellow, that faith apart from [good] works is <u>inactive and ineffective and worthless</u>?"*
> James 2:20, AMP

Real Bible faith will always have corresponding actions. If you believe and are saved, then you will act like it. Some of the things you used to do you won't do anymore. Some of the things you didn't do before, you will start doing. A saved person is a changed person. If you believe Jesus' gave Himself and took your poverty, then we will see corresponding actions. As you confess the Word and meditate on it, your capacity for faith in prosperity and abundance will increase. Your faith will grow.

You will need to also take corresponding actions to go along with your faith in God's blessings for you...

1) **Seek and Worship God.** Spend time seeking God. Spend time praying to Him and especially thanking Him for the wonderful blessings He has given you. Thank Him for the cross. Thank Him for your deliverance from poverty. Tell Him how much you love Him. Make God your first priority in life and seek to worship Him first. Everything else must take a backseat to your love and worship of Him.

2) **Quit Borrowing Money.** If you're in debt and believing God to get out of debt, then quit borrowing money for consumer debt. While borrowing money to buy real estate you invest in can increase your wealth, consumer debt such as credit card debt and vehicle loans will eat you alive. You may even need to go as far as we did and cut up all your credit cards. Debt has probably been a habit of yours for years, but you need to go cold turkey on it.

3) **Be Faithful in Your Job.** God rewards faithfulness. Show up to work on time. Do your job as unto the Lord. He is watching, so you're working at your job to please Him. Whether any person ever sees you or congratulates you, it doesn't matter. Show God you're a person who can be trusted to do the best job you can possibly do. Do what you can to bless your company.

4) **Cut Your Expenses.** If you are like most people, you've probably been wasting money in a lot of areas. What can you do to cut back? Cut down on going out to eat. Don't go to the movies. Put the 24 hour buying rule in place. Don't buy anything until you've thought about it for at least a day. Ask the Lord to show you other ways you can save money.

5) **Invest in Yourself.** There are only a few investments that always pay off. Investing your time and money in God is always a good investment. Investing in yourself is the other good investment. Go to the library and look for books which will help you improve and learn. Be willing to invest in books, CDs, and seminars. Your income will increase as you become more valuable and knowledgeable.

6) **Give.** Be a giver. If you haven't already become a giver, then use the Old Testament tithing of 10% as a starting point in your giving. You're not giving out of fear or with the motive of greed, but you know that you are lending to the Lord. You will never lack by being obedient to His commands and taking actions based on His Word and direction. If you don't become a giver now when you have little, you'll never become a giver just because you have abundance.

7) **Save.** In the future you will be saving excess money for investments and for things you want to purchase. While you're breaking the bondage of debt, the best thing you can do is save all of the extra money to pay off the debts quickly. Focus on paying off the credit cards, the cars, and even the home. Direct your money in this direction until you're completely out of debt. Once you're out of debt, you can begin purchasing things you may have gone without and putting more money into investments.

You are going to have to make sacrifices. It will probably be difficult for you at first. You begin believing God for financial freedom, and it seems like things are harder at first. You're cutting expenses and you're giving more. So it seems like you actually have less for a little while. Stay on track. It will only be a little while until the confession of your mouth and your new wise actions start producing a harvest in your life. Those debts will be put behind you and you will begin walking in God's abundance.

Focus on the Prize

> *"The sower soweth the word. And these are they by the way side, where the word is sown; but when they have heard, Satan cometh immediately, <u>and taketh away the word that was sown in their hearts</u>. And these are they likewise which are sown on stony ground; who, when they have heard the word, immediately receive it with gladness; And have no root in themselves, and so endure but for a time: afterward, when affliction or persecution ariseth for the word's sake, immediately they are offended."*
> Mark 4:14-17

The prize you're focusing on in your actions is financial freedom and financial abundance. You are looking towards the day when you are able to give large checks into the winning of more souls for the kingdom. You are looking towards the day when you don't have to save for months to buy a new set of furniture. You are looking forward to God's abundance in your life. Keep focused on that prize. Keep focused on God's Word to you.

Satan will come immediately to steal the Word just like He always does. He'll try to get you to ignore what you've been taught. He'll tell you another way to do it instead. He'll tell you to go back to your old ways. That is what Satan does and he is very good at his job. He is out to steal the Word of your deliverance from you. Don't let him take it. Fight back. Confess the Word. Read through this book a second or third time. Make it become a part of you.

If his tactics fail to steal the Word from you, he'll try sending affliction or persecution to you. He'll have people come to you who don't believe like you believe. He'll use them to discourage you. He'll use them to tell you how foolish you're being. They'll try to put you back in your little box of limited blessings. They'll tell you to quit rocking the boat. At the same time Satan will try to use afflictions and trials to shake your faith.

You're believing for financial abundance and he'll try to make something go wrong in your life such as the car breaking down or the washing machine quitting. Remember, he is after the Word. If he can get you off the Word, then he has you back in his hand. His goal is to get that Word out of you and he'll use any means necessary to get it. He'll use your brother or he'll use the broken down car. His one goal is to get you to quit obeying the Word.

After you beat him down, you'll begin to see victory in your life. You'll see God's blessing raining in. That is when the devil uses his most powerful tactics. He uses distractions to get you away from the Word. You couldn't buy anything before. Now you can buy all kinds of things. His goal now is to distract you from God's presence and will for your life. He'll jump on the bandwagon and be your buddy now. He is out to make you so comfortable and busy with other things that you neglect God and His will. Satan doesn't care how much money you have as long as you're not giving it to God. He doesn't care if you're not using it for God. So that's his purpose on this attack. More people have fell here than anywhere else. So be careful. You're no longer ignorant of the devil's devices.

Chapter Seventeen
Find Your Passion...and You'll Realize Your Purpose

> *"For I know the thoughts that I think toward you, saith the LORD, thoughts of peace, and not of evil, to give you an expected end."*
> Jeremiah 29:11

> *"For I know the thoughts and plans that I have for you, says the Lord, thoughts and plans for welfare and peace and not for evil, to give you hope in <u>your final outcome</u>."*
> Jeremiah 29:11, AMP

God has a purpose and a plan for you. People who are called to preach are not the only ones who are called of God. Being a business person is a call of God. One believer may be called to build and pastor a church of 2,000 people. They work. They delegate. They counsel. They preach. Another believer may be called to build a string of two dozen bakeries across the country. They're a witness of the goodness of God to those around them and a light in a dark world of business. They're also one of the primary givers supporting the church the pastor was called to work in.

The majority of people go though life without a dream and without a purpose to work towards. It's a dream and passion to fulfill it which gives you life and excitement. It's no wonder so many people deal with depression and anxiety. They're lacking focus and direction. If you don't know where you're going, any road will take you there. People turn to TV, alcohol, drugs, pornography, sex, etc. to find some excitement in their life.

Even born again people suffer with depression and boredom. Yes, God is the one who fills that lack in your life and

Find Your Passion...And You'll Realize Your Purpose

your heart. He is the only one who can give you unconditional love and acceptance which will set you free from the bondages of this world. He loves you exactly like you are, but He also loves you too much to leave you the way you are.

He sent us His Word to change us. We have already studied how you can meditate in the Bible and change your entire thinking pattern. You used to have grasshopper thinking, but He is transforming you into the champion you were created to be. He has a big purpose and plan for you. It isn't for you to just sit at home or go work at a dead-end job. It is something bigger than you have ever imagined before. It is a plan that will require you to grow, have faith, work hard, and rely on Him to help you every step along the way.

In Jeremiah 29:11, God says He is thinking about you. Isn't that something? God, creator of the heavens and the earth, is thinking about you. He hasn't forgotten you and He isn't ignoring you. He is thinking about you right this minute. What is He thinking about you? You may have thought God was thinking about how evil you used to be or how you screw up all the time. Maybe God was thinking about how disobedient you are or how useless you seem to be.

NO! It tells us exactly what God is thinking about you. He is thinking thoughts of peace about you...and not of evil. It also says He has plans for your welfare and peace...not for evil. He is thinking about you right now with thoughts of peace. I remember back to when I was dating my wife. I would sit there and think about her when I wasn't with her. I would sit there and just wish I could be next to her. We have been married for years and it still happens. If one of us is traveling and the other one is home, I count the days until we can be together again. I'm thinking thoughts of love toward her.

God is thinking thoughts of love and peace toward you. Not only that, but it says He is making plans for you and for your final outcome. He isn't just thinking about you, but He is also thinking about His plan for how He is getting you to your final purpose and calling. He has a plan for you, but you have to choose to work with Him on it. You are not an innocent bystander who just lets God do all the work. You are to work with Him at creating your destiny.

> *"But as for you, ye <u>thought evil against me; but God meant it unto good</u>, to bring to pass, as it is this day, to save much people alive."*
> Genesis 50:20

Joseph said this when his brothers came to him while he was managing all of Egypt. They had done evil to him. They had planned for him to be a slave and to rid themselves of the "dreamer." Yet with all the evil they had done, God continually took it and turned it around for good to reach Joseph's final outcome and purpose. No matter who stands against you or how they try to stop you, God can turn it around for good.

When Joseph was young, he dreamed about being a ruler. He caught the vision and inside he was a ruler. When he was sold into slavery, he was still a ruler inside and eventually became a ruler in the household he worked in. When he was put into prison, the heart of a ruler continued in him and he eventually managed all of the prison. Eventually that vision took him to ruling directly under Pharaoh over all of Egypt. Nothing could turn off the light in his vision and purpose.

If you'll establish this same kind of heart, then nothing can stop you. Right now God looks at you and sees a champion. You may not have been acting like much of a champion. Gideon was hiding behind a winepress when the angel called him a mighty man of God. God has more faith in you than you have in yourself. He sees a champion in you even when everyone around you simply sees an average Joe or a failure. God sees your final outcome, and it is finally time for you to start looking at a portion of the plan He has for you.

You need to catch a vision of what God sees in you and for you. You need to begin to see yourself the way God sees you. You've been judging yourself by what you've done up till now while God looks at what you will become. Everyone else looks at the outside of a person, but God looks at the heart. He sees your potential and He sees your future.

God Gives You the Desires of Your Heart

"Delight thyself also in the LORD; and he shall give thee the <u>desires of thine heart</u>."
Psalms 37:4

"Among whom also we all had our conversation in times past in the lusts of our flesh, fulfilling <u>the desires of the flesh and of the mind</u>; and were by nature the children of wrath, even as others."
Ephesians 2:3

If you delight yourself in the Lord, He will give you the desires of your heart. I've already mentioned this scripture and how it has two different ways people look at it. Let's go a little deeper into it. The Hebrew word of "delight" is the word, "anag" which simply means, "to be soft or pliable." If you become soft and pliable in the Lord, he will give you the desires of your heart.

You're to make yourself soft and pliable to the Lord. Allow Him to mold and shape you into the person He wants you to be. This would be the exact opposite of being hard-hearted and set in your ways. You need to be willing to allow the Lord to change you. When you're soft and pliable, He'll place the right desires in your heart. When you're open to Him, spending time in His Word, and living a life of worship, then whatever desires are in your heart came from Him.

Notice that I also quoted Ephesians 2:3 above because you have other desires in you besides ones that come from your heart. The flesh and your mind have desires. Your flesh has a desire for sins such as pride, lust, gluttony, laziness, etc. It has evil desires, and you'll have to learn to overcome the flesh for as long as you live on this earth. Your mind will also have all kinds of ideas of how and what you should be doing. It has the desire to rule over and control people. It has a desire to be seen as a bigshot to those around you.

The desire we're looking for in you doesn't come from your flesh or your mind. We're looking for the desire of your heart which God has placed inside you. Once we find that desire, we'll have a clue to your purpose and direction. We can then also come up with a game plan to begin moving toward your final outcome. If you don't know where you're going, you'll never be able to get on the right road.

What is it you wish you were really doing with your life? If you pick any career or business, what would you pick? If you could do it all over again, what would you be doing? Who is it that you admire and wish you were more like? Those you admire are often a clue to some of the desires which are in you.

If God came to you and said you could pray for your life to become anything you wanted, what is it you would ask for? Think about this for moment. You can pick the lifestyle you want. You can live where you want. You can do whatever job or business you want. You can vacation where you want. You're not being asked what other people want from you or what they want in life. How would you describe your perfect life to Him of what you want Him to do for you?

When you cut away all your thoughts or wishes about life, what is it that you really desire in your heart?

What Are You Passionate About?

> *"And when he had made a scourge of small cords, he drove them all out of the temple, and the sheep, and the oxen; and poured out the changers' money, and overthrew the tables; And said unto them that sold doves, Take these things hence; make not my Father's house an house of merchandise. And his disciples remembered that it was written, <u>The zeal</u> of thine house hath eaten me up."*
> John 2:15-17

Jesus was passionate about His Father's house. The Greek word here is "zelos." It is a zeal which was often used when referring to the jealousy of a husband. Any man is walking on some very dangerous ground when they start messing around with another man's wife. That man loves his wife and he is jealous over her. Proverbs 6:32-36 says that jealously is the rage of a man and he will not relent.

That is the kind of passion we're talking about here. We're talking about the same kind of passion a man has for his new bride (he should have it later also but many people allow that passion to cool over time). He is passionate about that woman. Don't mess with her and don't talk bad about her. She is the love of his life and that love will even blind him to real faults she may have. She is on his mind all the time.

One of the clues to your purpose is to find out what you're passionate about. What do you love to learn more about? What do you do with your spare time? What subject do you love to talk about to your friends…or what subject gets you to boil over to where you just have to say something about it?

The people who are most successful in life are those who are passionate about what they do. They're excited about getting up in the morning and going to work. They're excited about learning more about the subject they're working with. They're excited about what they do and their passion is noticed by those that work around them. If you've ever had the opportunity to work around someone who loves what they do, their joy is just contagious. Everyone feels better around them.

It is almost like the work they do isn't even work to them anymore. Get around a musician, a writer, a speaker, or a salesperson who loves what they do. They get in a "zone" where it becomes effortless to them. They love it. They've found their purpose and passion. Does this mean they love every element in what they do? No. That speaker may love the energy and excitement while they're on the stage, but the plane rides and hotel beds may become drudgery. The author may love to write, but the dealing with a publishing house and book signing tour wears them out on the 40th day.

They love the creative part of their job, because that is their passion. There are other things they deal with, but they can't wait to get back to show time. This is the kind of passion we're dealing with here. You have purpose and when you're doing it, you know it. There may be other things that come along with the passion that you have to deal with, but you know when you've hit your zone.

If you had enough money to live a comfortable life for the rest of your life, but you were required to pick a 40 hour a week job...what job would you pick? Think about this. You can pick anything even if you're not currently qualified for it. What kind of job would you pick if it wasn't about the money? Once you figure this out, then you can go to the next step and see if you can create something that earns an income for you.

It's a sad state of being for anyone to spend their life doing something they hate just to support a hobby they love. Surely you know someone like this. Maybe you're this person. We'll call this woman Sue. Sue is an accountant who works at a large accounting firm and often puts in 50 to 60 hour weeks. At tax time she'll work even more than this. She wakes up to the sound of the alarm clock in the morning and crawls out of bed. She barely makes it to the shower without falling back to sleep. She does her morning routine and waits in an hour of traffic to get to her job.

She does the paperwork and works with her clients all morning long until the lunch break. Every fifteen minutes has her staring at the clock wishing it would move just a little bit faster. She receives the wonderful news that this afternoon will have her working through an IRS audit with one of her most disliked clients. She has to prepare and only gets a short period for today's lunch. "What's new," she says to herself.

During the audit, she dazes in and out as the agent drones on and on as she shows them one document after another. The clock must hate her, because it seems to have slowed down time just to spite her. Finally, hallelujah, it's 5 PM, and it's over for the day. She races to her car and drives home as fast as the law allows. She walks to her house and is met by her excited door greeters. Both them and her have waited all day for this. Now she can relax.

She sits on the couch and collects up her 2 dogs and a cat. She gives them the attention they deserve and that she craves from her very being. She turns on "Animal Planet" and spends the rest of the evening cuddling with her critters and telling them about how awful her life is.

All week this daily pattern completes itself again and again. Sometimes she drops by the library and picks up books on dog training or she'll drop by the local animal shelter to help out. Saturdays is her day off and both her and the pets love this day. She gets to spend all day with them, train them, and take them to the park. It's the highlight of her existence.

I'll bet the story I just told you sounds very familiar. If it isn't about you, it is about someone you know. They do a job they hate just to have enough money to do a hobby they love. What should Sue be doing? If you've made it this far in this book, you should already have the answer. She should begin researching businesses that have to do with pets. She could be a dog trainer, write books about pets, open a dog bakery, have a pet store, be a dog groomer, open a kennel, be a pet sitter, etc. The only limitation is what she can come up with and imagine.

She doesn't have to quit her job to start doing those things. She can begin some of them and keep her job until she can replace her income. She could work in a business and eventually get to the point where she hires others to work for her as well...greatly multiplying her income. She'll still use her accounting skills to manage the finances from her new business. They don't go to waste. They just get applied to something much better.

There is so much opportunity all around us that no one has to spend their lives doing something they hate. It is simply comfort and fear which keeps you in the position you're in. I pray you become so uncomfortable where you're at that you have to make a change. Sue can make a change, but will she be willing to? How about you?

What Are You Talented At?

> *"And unto one he gave five talents, to another two, and to another one; to <u>every man according to his several ability</u>; and straightway took his journey."*
> Matthew 25:15

You have talents. God has given every man talents according to their ability. Don't sit there and tell me you haven't received any talents because I know you have. God says He gave talents to everyone. So you have talents...and I'll predict you have unused talents you don't even know about yet.

Some people become confused on what they're passionate about because they accepted someone else's vision of them. Your parents may have told you how cute you are and how wonderful you sing, so you've decided that is your passion and purpose. Well if you can't sing a note, then that is not your purpose. I've been in church where you're forced to suffer through some people singing every week until you simply can't stand it anymore. If your singing sounds like a bunch of cats have been put in a bag and are screeching as they're beaten with a stick, then please don't sing with the microphone again. That is not your calling.

Some preachers weren't called by God. Their mother called them or their father called them. All you have to do is sit down and listen to their confused droning for a few minutes, and you'll realize God didn't call them. If show time doesn't come with excitement and passion in you, then it is not your calling. Some preachers need to quit preaching and go into business. They missed their calling because they're following a calling given to them by someone other than God.

I'm talented at writing and speaking. I love it and am passionate about that. So I involve a lot of both in my business. I don't always love every part of my business, but I do enjoy those parts of the business. If you aren't talented at writing, then you don't want to put yourself in that business. I am not talented at singing or playing musical instruments. I've tried both, but it was not an enjoyable experience....for me or for those who had to listen to me. You'll never know where your talents lie until you try it. Many people are so afraid of trying something new and moving out of their comfort zone that they never find their talents.

Another question that comes up while looking at your talents is about what solutions you can provide people with. You won't make money just because you're good at something. You have to find something people are willing to pay you for. All jobs and business is based on becoming a solution to someone's problem. Even if you work at McDonald's, that is true. The problem is people are hungry and someone needs to cook the burger. The solution is you can do it.

What kind of problems have you solved or can you solve? All work is based around this factor. An evangelist solves the problem that people haven't heard the Gospel. The car dealer solves the problem that you need a way to get around. The airline solves the problem when you're in Florida and need to be in California by this evening. The real estate investor solves the problem that people need a place to live.

What kinds of problems can you solve with the talents you have or with the experience you've had in your life? Your first instinct may be to say you've never solved any problems. If you say that, you're just not thinking hard enough about the question. Pray and ask God to reveal to you situations and problems you've overcome or that you can help others in. Then keep your eyes and ears open to everything that goes on around you.

Once you really open your eyes to opportunities around you, you will be shocked. There are even people who are personal shoppers. That's a business where they do other people's shopping for them! Wealthy people often find themselves too busy to shop for clothing, furniture, groceries, or gifts. So they hire someone else to do it for them. There are personal shoppers who earn six figure incomes or even higher! So if shopping is your talent, this may be the business for you.

There are problems all around you, and you may either already have a solution or God can give you wisdom for the solution. All problems are an opportunity for someone to build a business and profit. You've just allowed yourself to be blinded to all the opportunities around you everyday. You've been afraid to step out and let your talents shine.

Finding God's Vision For You

"Where there is no vision, the people perish: but he that keepeth the law, happy is he."
Proverbs 29:18

"And the Lord said, Behold, they are one people and they have all one language; and this is only the beginning of what they will do, and now nothing they have imagined they can do will be impossible for them."
Genesis 11:6, *AMP*

If you don't have a vision, you perish. If you don't have a vision for your life, you slowly die inside. If there isn't hope to look forward to, you become hopeless and depressed. God built you with the desire to always be working and stretching toward goals in your life. You are made in God's image and He is the Creator. A creative nature has been built into you. You are not the Creator, but you are creative. Your heart desires to have a vision and goal to push towards.

Look at Genesis 11:6. God said that a group of people in unity could accomplish anything they imagined. Nothing was impossible for them. How much more is this true with God working with and blessing you in the desire He gave you! It was all based on their vision and plan. With a vision, anything was possible. That's why this whole chapter has been written to help you find a concentrated vision and plan for your life. Without a vision, you will perish. With a vision, nothing is impossible to you.

Find Your Passion...And You'll Realize Your Purpose

What is your current vision for your life? Have you been asking yourself all the questions throughout this chapter? Continue asking God for wisdom in revealing a vision to you for your life. If you're working a job, do you have a vision of going into business for yourself? If you already own a business, are you catching the vision of growth and expansion? If you currently have one store and are earning $100,000 a year net profit, do you see the vision of owning 10 stores earning $1,000,000 net profit?

You may only be able to give $100 offerings right now. Can you catch the vision of being able to give a one million dollar offering in the future? That's one of my visions. I can see the day I write million dollar checks to support the Gospel. Is that something you can imagine doing? If not, then you won't be doing it. If you can see it in your heart, then you can accomplish it through God.

Up until today, you've probably been told not to expect too much. You've probably trained yourself to be a small thinker. It's time to take the blinders off. It's time to become a big thinker. God hasn't put any limitations on you. With His help, no one else can limit you. So the only person who can limit you is yourself. Your vision of yourself and your future is the only limiting factor in your life.

"Jesus said unto him, If thou canst believe, all things are possible to him that believeth."
Mark 9:23

What things are possible with God? All things are possible. There is a condition here. It says that all things are possible to him who believes. If you don't believe, then it's not possible for you. If you say you can do it, you're right. If you say you can't do it, then you're right also. God's work and purpose in your life is based on your faith. Take this time to give Him something to work with.

What would you decide to do today if you knew you could not fail? You know you have desires you would step out on if the fear of failure didn't exist. If you knew everything would turn out alright, you would be doing something different in your life or business already. What is that change you're thinking of right now?

You know I'm telling you the truth. There have been times you've thought or even said, "I just wish..." You have unfulfilled desires from God in you. You've wished you were doing something different or you've wished to be able to do more than you are right now. The only thing which has been holding you back is a lack of vision and a lack of faith.

God has more for you to do. Now is your chance. Get to a quiet place. Ask God to sanctify your thoughts and desires. Then ask Him to show you the real desires of your heart and a vision of your future. It ought to scare you. If what you end up thinking about and seeing inside yourself isn't so big that it's scary, then you're probably holding yourself back with grasshopper thinking.

Your vision for your life should be so big that there is no way for you to accomplish it without God's help. It must require faith, because it is faith which pleases God (Hebrews 11:6). You haven't went far enough in your thinking until you say, "There is no way I could ever do that if God Himself didn't show up and help me!"

Once you're at the point where you know it's going to take God's help, then you're beginning the process where God can get to work with you. Up till now you've been working with your own pitiful human abilities. Now you're putting faith in God to work in your life. He has been waiting all this time for you to require His help!

Write Your Goals

> "And the LORD answered me, and said, <u>Write the vision, and make it plain</u> upon tables, that he may run that readeth it."
> Habakkuk 2:2

Having a vision and having a goal isn't enough. You also need to write them down. You have to write the vision and make it plain. Be specific in what you write. Get a piece of paper and write down the answers to some of the questions I've asked you throughout this chapter. Write down the answers to some of these questions:

> If God said you could pray for your life to become anything you wanted, what would you ask for?
>
> If you pick any career or business, what would you pick?
>
> Who is it that you admire and wish you were more like?
>
> What subject do you love to talk about to your friends?
>
> What are you passionate about?
>
> What talents do you have?
>
> What talents have other people said you have?
>
> What kind of problems can you solve?
>
> What would you do today if you could not fail?

Once you're finished going through those questions, let's take the next step. Now you're going to make a list of goals for your life. Some of the goals can be short-term such as something you can accomplish in the next few weeks or the next few months. Other ones should be goals that you want to accomplish before you die. If you're young, they may be 50 year goals. If you getting up in age, they may be 20 year goals.

The goals you're going to write down can be goals involving your career, your business, your marriage, your fitness, your children, your church, your character, your hobbies, your giving, or any other subject you want to create goals in.

They can be projects you want to accomplish. Think about all the things you would like to accomplish this year, this decade, and throughout your life. Once you've thought about it for a while. Then sit down and write.

Write 100 goals in the next 30 minutes. This will be hard work if you're not used to big planning and big thinking. I know it was hard for me when I first did this. I ended up with goals in all different categories such as giving a million dollar offering, training 1 million Christian businesspeople to be Champions for God, and weighing 170 pounds. I set specific income goals for my business...both short-term and long-term. I set goals for things I wanted to see change in my character and how I treated people around me. I wrote goals for projects I wanted to complete and things I wanted to accomplish.

You'll find that a lot of the things you've been thinking about and even direction in your life you've been confused about gets cleared up in the goal writing process. Personally I had heard other people talk about the value of writing goals, but I never realized how powerful it was until I applied it in my own life. Look back at the verse in Habakkuk 2:2. The Lord said to write the vision and make it plain. Writing your goals will make things in your life more plain to you. Everything you've been through and everything you've felt in your heart will simply make more sense to you.

Once you've finished your list and written all your goals, then read over the list you've made. Make sure all of the goals are specific. You don't want to lose weight. You want to lose 30 pounds. You don't want to increase your business. You want to increase your net profit by $55,000 this year. A general goal is not a goal at all. Be specific in your goal writing just like you need to be specific in your prayers.

Take it before the Lord in prayer and ask Him to give you wisdom about which goals should be most important to you right now. You should also begin praying now that the Lord reveal to you plans for you to accomplish some of the specific goals. Pick out 10 of the shorter term goals and make those your

Find Your Passion...And You'll Realize Your Purpose

goals you will concentrate on right now (watch as your faith grows when these get accomplished).

> *"Now <u>faith is the substance of things hoped for</u>, the evidence of things not seen."*
> Hebrews 11:1

Faith is the substance of things hoped for. We're going to take those 10 primary goals you picked and apply faith to them. Write them as if they were already done now. For example, one of your goals may say, "My business will earn $100,000 net profit this year." Change it to say, "My business earns $100,000 per year." Make it present tense. You may have a goal which says, "I want to weigh 120 pounds." Change it to, "I now weigh 120 pounds."

Faith is always in the present tense. Now take each of those goals and see yourself having it now. Use the power of your God given imagination to see yourself making the money you want to earn, acting the way you've decided to act, and weighing whatever you decided to weigh. If your goal was to be someone who edifies and builds others up instead of gossiping, see yourself talking well about others to those around you.

Keep this list handy. Pray over it. Go over it everyday. Say it out loud and see it taking place in your life. Thank God for working your life and accomplishing all of these things. Praise Him for His goodness. Let faith go to work in your life. Finally you've given God something He can work with. As small goals are accomplished, other goals from your big list can be added in. Your faith will increase as you see these things come to pass in your life.

Make a Plan

> *"For which of you, intending to build a tower, <u>sitteth not down first, and counteth the cost</u>, whether he have sufficient to finish it? Lest haply, after he hath laid the foundation, and is not able to finish it, all that behold it*

begin to mock him, Saying, This man began to build, and was not able to finish. Or what king, going to make war against another king, <u>sitteth not down first, and consulteth</u> whether he be able with ten thousand to meet him that cometh against him with twenty thousand? Or else, while the other is yet a great way off, he sendeth an ambassage, and desireth conditions of peace."
Luke 14:28-32

Once you've made your goals, you now need to count the cost. You'll never accomplish anything in life without paying a cost for it. To build a business will require you to work longer hours in the beginning. You may have to get up early or stay up later. You may have to banish your TV for the next year. If you want to save more money, you may have to quit going out to eat so often. You may have to cut out some of your shopping budget.

If you plan to study and learn new subjects for your personal growth, you may have to turn off the radio station and listen to training CDs on the way to work. Anything you do for God, for your family, or for yourself will cost a price. It may be not as high of a price as you would think, but it will cost you something. For example, anyone can become an expert in virtually any subject in just one hour a day study over a year to two year period. That is a lot easier than most people would think, but it is still an hour which has to be invested everyday.

Count the cost for your goals. Make a plan. You should never start a new business without a plan, and you'll never reach your goals without a plan either. You may want to weigh 30 pounds less than you do right now, but how do you plan to accomplish this? When will you schedule to exercise and what kind of exercise will you do? How will you change your eating habits to cut your daily calories? How can you get your friends or family to help you on this goal?

You can pick up dozens of books at any bookstore on the subject of losing weight. The hidden little secret is that the majority of them work, because you simply need to exercise

Find Your Passion...And You'll Realize Your Purpose

more and cut the number of calories you eat. So you don't have to starve yourself or go on any crazy fad diet. Just make a plan that includes both exercise and diet.

Make your plan by breaking down the goal into elements or steps. What kinds of steps will you have to take to reach your goal? The number of steps you use will be based on how complicated of a goal you have. If you're starting a new business, you may have dozens of steps to prepare. You need to study the marketplace, visit competitors, do customer research, etc. Then you need to apply for licenses, setup a legal business form such as corporation, and possibly apply for business loans based on a business plan you've written.

If your long-term plan is to build your current business to $1,000,000 a year in net profits, then you may have one year goal and plan for $100,000 increase. For that plan, you may make a list of asking customers why they buy from you, writing new ads, testing your ads, and checking around to find joint venture partners who may be able to offer more items to your current customers.

You can break down these plans into many more steps than what I've listed here. The planning stage should be broken down into easy to accomplish daily and weekly goals. When I said write a new ad above, that could be broken down into individual steps as well. You may design 3 ads to test, so you first decide on the "offer" for each one...what will make it unique and exciting to your customers. Then you decide on headlines. Then you write the rough draft of one ad. Then you edit it. Then you test it. Then you see if you can improve on it or test out one of the other possible offers you come up with.

The other important element that comes in while making plans is to make deadlines that are practical. You may want to lose 30 pounds, but doing that in 30 days is not practical. You will not reach that goal and do it in a healthy fashion. The healthiest way to lose weight is 1 to 2 pounds per week. So your goal may be to lose 30 pounds in the next 6 months. Then you can break that down further and say you would like to lose 5 pounds this month. You didn't gain 30 pounds in a month, and you won't be losing it in one month either. So make shorter term goals such as losing 5 pounds per month.

If the most you've ever made in your life is $30,000 per year, then having a goal of making one million this year is not a realistic goal. Making one million in a year 5 to 10 years from now definitely would be something you can accomplish with God's help, but you'd be better off setting a goal of $60,000 or so for your business. You then would need to come up with all the steps required for you to reach that goal. If it's a brand new business you're starting, there will be a lot of steps involved. Pick up several books that talk about starting new businesses to help you write down all the steps you'll need to take. Then get busy and start taking one step at a time.

One of the key principles here is you want your goals to be something you can really have faith in. You are only limited by what you can believe, but you won't be able to believe with your heart that you're worth the one million dollar income if you've only been making $30,000. You're going to have to grow into it. You'll have to build up to the point where you truly believe you're worth that much money.

Most people set their one year goals too high and their 5 year goals too low. You can experience multiplied growth every year of your life, so your goals for 5 years out should be a whole lot bigger than your goals for this year alone. God wants to help you build the life you dream about, but you have to be willing to put in both the time and energy required to get there. You have a lot of learning and growing to do.

Look at potential roadblocks which may come up in the pursuit of your goal. What kind of obstacles are likely to come against you? This is part of counting the cost. You may have friends who won't want to be around you anymore. People who are set in their ways and satisfied with mediocre life don't usually accept those who want to strive for excellence. If you want to soar with the eagles, you might not be close friends with the turkeys anymore. You may have opposition from your family. Jesus said people from your own household will become your opposition (Matthew 10:36).

You are an overcomer and God will help you defeat any roadblock or opposition which comes against you. Just like the king who was going to war, you must count the cost. Look at some of the potential obstacles, pray about them, and decide today that you will overcome them. Your path to greatness will come with giants who stand in your way. How could you ever be declared the champion if you didn't have competition to overcome?

Find Knowledgeable Christians for Counsel

> "*Without counsel purposes are disappointed: but in the multitude of counsellors they are established.*"
> Proverbs 15:22

If you go it alone, you may end up disappointed. You need advice and you need support. Find other believers who can encourage you and help you. Purposes are established by a multitude of counselors. We're not just talking about any kind of counselor either. Your current friends may not be good counselors for you. You'll have a hard time getting counsel on starting a business from anyone who hasn't owned their own successful business. You don't want to be taking advice from people who don't have faith in God or you.

If you want to lose weight, don't ask for advice from someone who weighs more than you. Everyone has an opinion about everything, and most of them are wrong! Find someone around you who has lost the weight and kept it off. They can provide both counsel and support to you. Pick up books you can gain advice and inspiration from as well. Surround yourself with positive information and tools which can help you reach your goals.

If you already have a business and want to improve on it, don't just hang around people who do about the same as you and are satisfied with it. Look to associate with those who want improvements in every area of their business. Pick up materials that show you how to improve your marketing, decrease your time expense, and work better with your employees. Be willing to hire a consultant or coach who can help you improve your business as well. Often someone outside the company will see multiple ways to improve your business immediately just because they have a more broad viewpoint to see it from.

I constantly educate myself in every area of business. I buy both books and courses. I attend seminars. I've hired coaches and consultants. Every penny I've ever spent in educating myself has always come back multiplied. I consider the money I've spent on personal education as the best money I've ever invested. You need to gain that attitude as well. Having someone who can help you come up with the steps you need to reach your goal is invaluable. Wisdom is the principal thing. Wisdom is simply having knowledge and knowing how to apply it to your daily life.

One caution to take in finding counsel is you will want to work with counselors who are Christian. No matter what your goals are, you want to make sure they are focused on God. For example, you wouldn't want a consultant to teach your entire sales force to lie to your customers for more business. You also wouldn't want them to recommend anything illegal or dishonest in any area of business. If you're looking for a Christian who is an experienced business coach to help you improve profits or decrease expenses, please feel free to contact my office. You can find out more about what we offer at: http://www.mymarketingcoach.com..

Take Action Today

"But wilt thou know, O vain man, that faith without works is dead?"
James 2:20

You've established a vision. You've written your goals. You've made a step-by-step plan to where you need to go. You've found Christian counsel who has gone before you. Now you have to take action. Faith without works is dead. If you

Find Your Passion...And You'll Realize Your Purpose

don't start immediately taking action, then all the goal setting has been in vain. You need to start doing the steps on each of your goal lists today. Don't just pray and expect God to do it all for you. That's not faith. That's hope. Faith takes action.

Faith gets moving. Faith takes risks. Creating a plan and having counsel is vital to this process, but there comes a day when you must begin the plan. You can't just sit around imagining your goals, confessing the Word, and expect things to change. The Word was given to change you. You have to step out in faith and change the circumstances around you.

"Now when they had gone throughout Phrygia and the region of Galatia, and were <u>forbidden</u> of the Holy Ghost to preach the word in Asia, After they were come to Mysia, they <u>assayed to go into Bithynia</u>: but the Spirit suffered them not."
Acts 16:6-7

This is about Paul and the people who traveled with him. They went through Phrygia and Galatia. They were going to go to Asia, but the Holy Spirit stopped them. Then they were going to Bithynia, and the Holy Spirit stopped them again. What I want you to see here is that Paul was always moving. He was always pushing forward in faith. He didn't sit around waiting for the Lord to give him a push. The Holy Spirit didn't have to inspire him to go. The Holy Spirit had to tell him when to stop!

Most believers are exactly the opposite of this. We want to wait until everything is perfect and everyone agrees with us before we take any action. God is continually trying to drag us kicking and screaming to success. We have our feet dug in and are resisting the whole way. Once everything lines up perfectly, then we decide it is time to go. If most of us were in Paul's shoes, we would be thoroughly convinced we weren't called...especially on the days where he was beaten with whips and thrown in jail.

Yet he accomplished ministering the Gospel around a majority of Rome at the time. He also wrote two-thirds of the

New Testament. He did this while being "part-time" in the ministry. He made and sold tents to support himself. He was a man with big visions and big goals. He was also a man who had a plan and was willing to take action to get there. He was constantly taking action. The Lord would tell him when it was time to stop instead of when it was time to go.

You need to start stepping out into the same type of faith. God has already spoken His Word and it will not change. He has already said He has given you the power to get wealth. He has already promised that with faith nothing shall be impossible to you. It's time for you to start taking action based on what God has already said. It is time for you to become one of God's champions and change the world around you!

Chapter Eighteen
Meditate in the Word

"Blessed is the man that walketh not in the counsel of the ungodly, nor standeth in the way of sinners, nor sitteth in the seat of the scornful. But his delight is in the law of the LORD; and in his law doth he <u>meditate day and night</u>. And he shall be like a tree planted by the rivers of water, that bringeth forth his fruit in his season; his leaf also shall not wither; and <u>whatsoever he doeth shall prosper</u>."
Psalms 1:1-3

Your delight should be in the Word of God. You can meditate in it day and night. If you do, you will be like a tree planted by the rivers of water. You will bring forth fruit in its season. Your leaf will not wither. Everything you do will prosper! God has revealed the secret of prospering in everything you do. You simply have to meditate in the Word day and night. Prosperity is inevitable.

Meditation involves saying and seeing. You speak the Word out loud and you see it taking place in your mind. You see yourself as a doer of the Word. Talk about prosperity. See prosperity in your life. Take special times where you close off the world and just meditate in the Word. In addition to those specific times, change your vocabulary. Fill your mouth with the Word of God. You should get to the place in your life where the Word of God comes to mind first no matter what the situation.

This bonus chapter has been added for your convenience. Many prosperity scriptures can be found here for you to begin meditating. Beneath each one is also a personalized version for you to read off to yourself. All the prosperity passages are obviously not included. These are to be a starting point for you in your meditation. Let the Lord lead you to other ones He may have for you.

"For ye know the grace of our Lord Jesus Christ, that, though he was rich, yet for your sakes he became poor, that ye through his poverty might be rich."
2 Corinthians 8:9

I know the grace of my Lord Jesus Christ. Though he was so very rich, he became poor for my sake. Through his poverty I have been made rich and abundantly supplied.

"But thou shalt remember the LORD thy God: for it is he that giveth thee power to get wealth, that he may establish his covenant which he sware unto thy fathers, as it is this day."
Deuteronomy 8:18

God gives me power to get wealth to establish His covenant.

"And God is able to make all grace abound toward you; that ye, always having all sufficiency in all things, may abound to every good work:"
2 Corinthians 9:8

God has given me grace and divine favor. I always have everything I need and I have abundance to give into all good works.

"And he shall be like a tree planted by the rivers of water, that bringeth forth his fruit in his season; his leaf also shall not wither; and whatsoever he doeth shall prosper."
Psalms 1:3

I'm like a tree planted by the rivers of water. I bring forth fruit in my season. My leaf does not wither, and whatever I do will prosper.

"A good man leaveth an inheritance to his children's children: and the wealth of the sinner is laid up for the just."
Proverbs 13:22

I am leaving an inheritance to my grandchildren. The wealth of the sinner has been saved up for me.

"Beloved, I wish above all things that thou mayest prosper and be in health, even as thy soul prospereth."
3 John 2

God wishes above all things that I prosper and be in health, even as my soul is prospering.

"If any of you lack wisdom, let him ask of God, that giveth to all men liberally, and upbraideth not; and it shall be given him."
James 1:5

I have asked God for wisdom so He is pouring His wisdom liberally into me everyday.

"Let them shout for joy, and be glad, that favour my righteous cause: yea, let them say continually, Let the LORD be magnified, which hath pleasure in the prosperity of his servant."
Psalms 35:27

I shout for joy and am glad. I say continually, Let the Lord be magnified. He has pleasure in my prosperity.

"The thief cometh not, but for to steal, and to kill, and to destroy: I am come that they might have life, and that they might have it more abundantly."
John 10:10

Satan comes to steal, kill, and to destroy. Jesus came so I could have abundant life.

"And he sought God in the days of Zechariah, who had understanding in the visions of God: and as long as he sought the LORD, God made him to prosper."
2 Chronicles 26:5

As long as I seek the Lord, He'll make me prosper.

"By humility and the fear of the LORD are riches, and honour, and life."
Proverbs 22:4

I'm humble and fear the Lord. I receive riches, honor, and life.

"He that giveth unto the poor shall not lack: but he that hideth his eyes shall have many a curse."
Proverbs 28:27

I give to the poor. I shall never lack.

"The blessing of the LORD, it maketh rich, and he addeth no sorrow with it."
Proverbs 10:22

God's blessings make me rich. He adds no sorrow to them.

"The thoughts of the diligent tend only to plenteousness; but of every one that is hasty only to want."
Proverbs 21:5

I'm a diligent person. My thoughts lead me only to abundance.

"Honour the LORD with thy substance, and with the firstfruits of all thine increase: So shall thy barns be filled with plenty, and thy presses shall burst out with new wine."
Proverbs 3:9-10

I honor the Lord with my possessions. I give him the firstfruits of all my income. My bank accounts are filled with plenty and my work bursts out with profits.

"Seest thou a man diligent in his business? he shall stand before kings; he shall not stand before mean men."
Proverbs 22:29

I am diligent in my business. I will stand before kings and not obscure men.

"If ye be willing and obedient, ye shall eat the good of the land:"
Isaiah 1:19

I am willing and obedient. I eat the good of the land.

"The rich ruleth over the poor, and the borrower is servant to the lender."
Proverbs 22:7

I serve no one but God. He has set me free from all debt and bondage.

"A faithful man shall abound with blessings: but he that maketh haste to be rich shall not be innocent."
Proverbs 28:20

I am a faithful man. I abound with blessings.

"But of him are ye in Christ Jesus, who of God is made unto us wisdom, and righteousness, and sanctification, and redemption:"
1 Corinthians 1:30

I am in Christ Jesus. He is my wisdom, my righteousness, my sanctification, and my redemption.

"Christ hath redeemed us from the curse of the law, being made a curse for us: for it is written, Cursed is every one that hangeth on a tree:"
Galatians 3:13

Christ has redeemed me from the curse of the law.

"The righteous shall flourish like the palm tree: he shall grow like a cedar in Lebanon. Those that be planted in the house of the LORD shall flourish in the courts of our God. They shall still bring forth fruit in old age; they shall be fat and flourishing;"
Psalms 92:12-14

I flourish like a palm tree. I grow like a cedar in Lebanon. I flourish in the courts of God. I will still bring forth fruit in old age. I will be full of vitality and life.

"He becometh poor that dealeth with a slack hand: but the hand of the diligent maketh rich."
Proverbs 10:4

My diligence will make me rich.

"But my God shall supply all your need according to his riches in glory by Christ Jesus."
Philippians 4:19

My God supplies all my need according to His riches in glory by Christ Jesus.

"In the house of the righteous is much treasure: but in the revenues of the wicked is trouble."
Proverbs 15:6

There is much treasure in my house because I have been made righteous.

"For verily I say unto you, That whosoever shall say unto this mountain, Be thou removed, and be thou cast into the sea; and shall not doubt in his heart, but shall believe that those things which he saith shall come to pass; he shall have whatsoever he saith."
Mark 11:23

I can speak to mountains and they have to obey. Whatever I say will come to pass, because I have whatever I say.

"Therefore I say unto you, What things soever ye desire, when ye pray, believe that ye receive them, and ye shall have them."
Mark 11:24

I receive whatever I desire and pray for, because I believe I receive when I pray.

"But without faith it is impossible to please him: for he that cometh to God must believe that he is, and that he is a rewarder of them that diligently seek him."
Hebrews 11:6

I please God by faith. I seek God diligently and He is my rewarder.

"This book of the law shall not depart out of thy mouth; but thou shalt meditate therein day and night, that thou mayest observe to do according to all that is written therein: for then thou shalt make thy way prosperous, and then thou shalt have good success."
Joshua 1:8

The Word of God does not depart out of my mouth. I meditate in it day and night. I do everything written in it. It makes my way prosperous and I have good success.

"The LORD is my shepherd; I shall not want. He maketh me to lie down in green pastures: he leadeth me beside the still waters. He restoreth my soul: he leadeth me in the paths of righteousness for his name's sake. Yea, though I walk through the valley of the shadow of death, I will fear no evil: for thou art with me; thy rod and thy staff they comfort me. Thou preparest a table before me in the presence of mine enemies: thou anointest my head with oil; my cup runneth over. Surely goodness and mercy shall follow me all the days of my life: and I will dwell in the house of the LORD for ever."
Psalms 23

The LORD is my shepherd; I shall not want. He makes me to lie down in green pastures: he leads me beside the still waters. He restores my soul: he leads me in the paths of righteousness for his name's sake. Yes, though I walk through the valley of the shadow of death, I will fear no evil: for thou art with me; thy rod and thy staff they comfort me. You prepare a table before me in the presence of my enemies: you anoint my head with oil; my cup runs over. Surely goodness and mercy shall follow me all the days of my life: and I will dwell in the house of the LORD forever.

About the Author

Terry Dean is the president of MyMarketingcoach, LLC. He is the author of several books and numerous audio and video sets. He is a business coach, author, and speaker. He has coached numerous businesses on how to dramatically increase their profits while cutting their overhead and increasing their time off.

He works one-on-one with business owners and through Mastermind groups of several business owners working together to all increase their profits. If you own a business or are considering starting one, then you should visit his coaching site today. You can find information on coaching, our free newsletter, and details on our many products designed to help you in your business.

http://www.mymarketingcoach.com

Free Newsletter:
http://www.mymarketingcoach.com

One-On-One Coaching:
http://www.mymarketingcoach.com/coaching/index.html

Speaking Topics for Conventions And Meetings:
http://www.mymarketingcoach.com/speaking/index.html

Business Training Products:
http://www.mymarketingcoach.com/products/index.html

Media Room:
http://www.mymarketingcoach.com/media/index.html

Terry Dean Business Blog:
http://www.terrydean.org

Are You Ready to Dramatically Increase Your Profits While Decreasing Your Time At Work…By Working With Your Own Personal One-On-One Christian Business Coach?

Is your business really fulfilling your goals spiritually, personally, and financially? Or is it simply exhausting you both physically and spiritually while not giving you the return on your investment that you have been hoping for? Running a business can be lonely, frustrating work…if you try to go it alone.

Sure you could talk to your employees or other members of your church, but they rarely understand the pressures that an entrepreneur faces each day. Nor do they have any idea how to help you with the problems coming against you. You need a coach who can help you in all the major problem areas your business faces each day.

We can help you:
- Get More Customers in the Door
- Better Serve Your Customers to Keep them Coming Back
- Maximize Profits
- Hire and train good employees
- Systematize your business so you can take more time off

We can help you **make your business better**. We will help you become the business owner that you **know** you can be.

Contact us today:
http://www.mymarketingcoach.com

"Without counsel purposes are disappointed: but in the multitude of counsellors they are established."
Proverbs 15:22

FREE Report...

"10 Key Strategies for Any Business Owner to Earn More, Work Less, and Enjoy Life!"

What if you could increase your profits exponentially without increasing your workload? What if the marketing you're already doing could be made 2 times...3 times...or even 5 times more effective without spending a single extra penny? Don't you owe it to yourself to find out what you could do to double or even triple the profits of your business in the next 30 days...especially since this report is totally FREE?

- How to **find your unique gifts and talents**...and how you can use them to create a dominating presence in any business marketplace.
- How to generate new leads and customers in your business...and **the real truth** about why so many businesses find this so difficult!
- The #1 key to building a business that doesn't require you to operate it...and how to **increase your income while taking more time off!**
- Why most **real money is made when you're on vacation** or relaxing...and how to put this success principle into action more often!
- How to build customer "evangelists" for your business...and let them constantly **do your marketing work for you!**

Pick up your free report today by visiting our web site at:

http://www.mymarketingcoach.com

Are You Looking for an Exciting, Entertaining Speaker for Your Next Workshop, Conference, or Church Meeting?

Schedule Terry Dean for your next event if you're ready for your attendees to have a change in their finances or in their businesses. Terry's presentations are both interactive and fun for all those involved. Below is a listing of some of his available speaking topics:

Marketing Mastery: How to Increase the Profits of Any Business Using Marketing With Integrity

How Any Business Can Profit From the Internet in Just 4 Easy Steps

Business Secrets of the Bible: How to Build Your Business Using God's Wisdom Revealed Thousands of Years Ago

God's Champions: Are You Satisfied With a Mediocre Life or Are You Ready to Become The Champion You've Been Created to Be?

Passion into Profits: How to Create the Life You Desire By Turning Your Life Purpose Into Your Business

Schedule Terry Dean for your next event by contacting us through our web site at:

http://www.mymarketingcoach.com/speaking.html

Spread the Message of Financial Freedom to Your Congregation, Your Friends, or Your Customers!

Discounted Bulk Orders of 10 or more are now available for…

"Financial Freedom: A Step-By-Step Practical Guide for Walking in God's Blessings!"

By Terry Dean
ISBN: 0-9762068-0-3

Don't keep this vital message to yourself. God desires to prosper His children, yet many of them are living in poverty and lack. Spread the message of freedom and faith in God's blessings to those in your congregation, your friends, or your customers. Many people talk about financial blessings, but this is one of the first books to actually draw out a step-by-step roadmap to receiving and walking in God's blessings everyday of your life.

Order 10 or more and receive a very special price on this book. Have one to give away to new church members, friends or family you know who are struggling with financial issues, and to couples who are just getting married. Make it available in your church bookstore or as a gift to members of your church.

http://www.mymarketingcoach.com/bulkorder.html

"But thou shalt remember the LORD thy God: for it is he that giveth thee power to get wealth, that he may establish his covenant which he sware unto thy fathers, as it is this day."
Deuteronomy 8:18

Printed in the United States
103530LV00001B/345/A